DEAR FELLOW MEMBER:

I count it a privilege to send you this copy of *Rainbows for God's Children in the Storm* by our beloved colleague Henry G. Bosch. Please accept it as my way of saying thank you for your support of Radio Bible Class.

In his 26 years as Executive Editor of *Our Daily Bread,* Henry has written more than one thousand articles for the purpose of bringing comfort and encouragement to Christians in the crucible of suffering. This book is a compilation of the best of those articles as they appeared in the devotional guide.

I trust that these meditations will bring blessing and help to you just as they have to millions of *Our Daily Bread* readers down through the years.

Richard W. DeHaan

Teacher, Radio Bible Class

Rainbows

for God's Children in the Storm

by Henry G. Bosch

ACKNOWLEDGMENTS

Ackley, A. H., © Renewal 1941. The Rodeheaver Co. p. 127
Miles, C. Austin, © Renewal 1962. The Rodeheaver Co. p. 175
Peterson, John W., © 1952. Norman Clayton Publishing Co. p. 92
Peterson, John W., © 1958. Singspiration, Inc. p. 97
Smith, Oswald J., © Renewal 1965. The Rodeheaver Co. p. 80
Weigle, C.F., © Renewal 1960. The Rodeheaver Co. p. 101

RAINBOWS
for God's Children in the Storm

Contents

Foreword

I am especially pleased that this volume is being added to the many already published by the Radio Bible Class in its more than four decades of ministry.

The articles in *Rainbows—for God's Children in the Storm* first appeared in the monthly issues of *Our Daily Bread,* and therefore have already ministered to the spiritual needs of many people throughout the world. I am confident that these specially chosen devotionals, now combined under this title, will bring multiplied blessings to all who read them.

It also gives me great personal satisfaction to see this book come to completion since it is the work of our beloved Henry Bosch. Because of his own personal experience, he is eminently qualified to write about God's comfort for the suffering. I have been working with Henry for more than a quarter of a century, and I can testify to his deep love for the Lord and his sensitivity to the needs of others. He writes from his heart!

Then too, it is fitting that we release such a volume in conjunction with the 25th anniversary of *Our Daily Bread,* the devotional guide which was conceived by and has continued all these years under the direction of "HGB."

We thank God for this compilation, and we pray that these meditations will produce rainbows of encouragement amid your storm clouds of trial and adversity.

"Blessed be God, even the Father of our Lord Jesus Christ, the Father of mercies, and the God of all comfort, who comforteth us in all our tribulation, that we may be able to comfort them who are in any trouble, by the comfort with which we ourselves are comforted of God" (2 Cor. 1:3,4).

Richard W. De Haan

Preface

During 25 years as editor of *Our Daily Bread*, I've written more than 1,000 meditations on the subject of comfort. The compilation of articles in this book constitutes a cross section of the various aspects of adversity, sorrow, trial, and difficulty that often cast a shadow on the believer's path. Through these meditations and some new material, I hope to bring consolation to all who may be troubled and fearful.

The Savior has taught me many blessed lessons in the school of affliction. Therefore, I welcome this opportunity to pass on to you a few of the grace notes from the songs of victory the Lord has given me in my night of trial. I can testify that in every threatening cloud of adversity the soul that trusts in Jesus can find His promised rainbow of hope! Like the cheerful robin, faith sings its sweetest song in the rain, knowing that each droplet of distress is part of a shower of spiritual refreshing (Rom. 8:28).

To Christians who seek the comfort of God (Rom. 15:4), I send this book on its way with a prayer that the Holy Spirit will indeed use it to pour the balm of Gilead into many wounded hearts.

> *Troubled? wait not in your woe,*
> *But at once to Jesus go;*
> *He the darkest clouds can make*
> *Hues of rainbow brightness take.*

Warmly and sympathetically,

Henry G. Bosch

Henry G. Bosch

1. Adversity and Trial

In Hebrews 12:11 we read, "Now no chastening for the present seemeth to be joyous, but grievous; nevertheless, afterward it yieldeth the peaceable fruit of righteousness unto them who are exercised by it." The two key words in this text are "exercised" and "afterward." God's glorious promise of the "peaceable fruit of righteousness" is contingent upon our being changed for the better by the trials and chastenings which come from God's loving hand. The way we are to be trained and made more spiritual is carefully outlined in the preceding verses of Hebrews 12. We are told that we must patiently, submissively, uncomplainingly, and courageously endure without faltering, no matter what the Lord sends into our lives. We can do this only as we recognize that He never sends anything to hurt us, but only to bless. He seeks to remove from us the sin and carnality that hinder our growth in grace. Heaven-sent trials and adversity are therefore the honor badges of membership in the family of God! "For whom the Lord *loveth* He chasteneth, and scourgeth every *son* whom He receiveth" (Heb. 12:6).

As we try to discern what God is teaching us

through our distresses, and as we become more obedient, we can expect the blessings of His rewarding "afterward." In this life it includes a deep settled peace and a newfound joy in seeing the fruit of the Spirit in our lives. We will grow rich by our losses, rise by our falls, and live by our dying.

Spurgeon rightly observed: "Our sorrows, like the passing keels of vessels upon the sea, leave a silver line of holy light behind them 'afterward.'" In keeping with that thought, an unknown poet has written:

God has a shining "afterward" for every cloud of rain;
We may not see the meaning now of sorrow and of pain;
Yet nothing God allows to come can ever be in vain;
The seed, if watered by our tears, becomes the golden
grain.

When affliction comes, do not expect to understand immediately what the Lord is teaching us. As one of the church fathers has observed, "Our Lord is much like a great Printer who sets the letters backward; we see and feel His setting, but we shall read the print much better in the life to come." Let's be content that our great and good Shepherd is up ahead in all the tomorrows, and that nothing comes to us unless it first passes through Him. Because of this, we can give thanks in trials. The weak Christian cries, "When am I going to get out of my troubles?" The spiritual believer asks, "What am I going to get out of them?"

Yes, the pruning of the divine Husbandman may be sharp and painful, but He knows what He's doing. So let's cling to His infallible promise which assures us that today's bitter experience will yield tomorrow's "peaceable fruit of righteousness."

In full assurance of faith may we declare with the undaunted courage provided by His grace:

I know the heights for which I long
Must oft be reached by cutting pain,
Though frosts of ill may try my soul,
The rainbow will be seen again! —Anon.

10

TREASURES IN DARK CLOUDS

Lo, I come unto thee in a thick cloud.   Exodus 19:9
And I will give thee the treasures of darkness.   Isaiah 45:3

CHRISTIANS often learn more in times of darkness and trial than in the pleasant sunlight of prosperity. God may be shrouded in a thick, impenetrable cloud when He has something very important to teach us. Yet we will not enjoy the treasures of His grace until we master the lessons He brings us in those gloomy days of distress. Even when we feel utterly forsaken, God is near. We ought to approach our difficulties without flinching. Beyond the blackness of our most severe trial, God's special blessing awaits us.

An unknown poet, thinking of troubles that sweep over us like raging storms, has written:

Hast thou a cloud?
A trial that is terrible to see?
A black temptation threatening thee?
A loss of some dear loved one long thine own?
A mist, a veiling, bringing the unknown?
A mystery unsolvable, it seems?
A cloud between thee and the sun's bright beams?
God cometh in that cloud!

A Christian sat near the peak of a high mountain, watching a storm as it raged below. Suddenly an eagle soared up through the clouds toward the sun — its pinions glistening like diamonds. The man thought to himself, had it not been for the tempest, that bird might have been content to remain in the valley. The same is true of believers. The sorrows of life cause us to rise toward God, where we see His grace in a new and refreshing light. This more than compensates for the momentary distress of our dark trials.

Ye fearful saints, fresh courage take;
The clouds ye so much dread
Are big with mercy, and shall break
In blessings on your head.   —Cowper

THOT: Beyond each cloud of trial is the rainbow of God's grace.

11

A STIRRED-UP NEST

As an eagle stirreth up her nest . . . , so the Lord
alone did lead him.   Deuteronomy 32:11,12

THE eagle always builds her nest in the tallest trees or on the loftiest mountain ledges. Someone who has observed this majestic bird constucting her home says that she first lays down *briers, jagged stones, and all kinds of sharp objects* which would seem to be unsuited for her purpose. She then covers this structure with a thick layer of wool, feathers, and the fur of animals she has killed. This makes the nesting place soft and comfortable—a delightful sanctuary where she may hatch her young. But the eaglets will not remain in their inviting cradle for long. The day will come when the mother will stir up the nest. With her sharp talons she will tear away some of the soft, downy lining so that her little ones will feel the sharp edges underneath. Up to this time, their food has been dropped into their mouths, but now the young birds become so miserable that they are willing to get out and begin looking for their own. This is the mother's objective. She is not being cruel, but is instinctively producing discontent with the old life of ease and spurring them on to full development.

This is a picture of how the Lord promotes the growth of His children. He often sends the barbs of adversity to rouse us from our complacency so that we may learn to lift our souls heavenward and move on to maturity in Christ. Strength comes from struggle; weakness from ease. If the sharp thorns and flinty stones of affliction are irritating you, it is God's grace designed to activate you! *A stirred-up nest is a token of His special love.* So spread your wings of faith and soar to new heights of blessing!

> *Higher, higher! blessed Holy Spirit,*
> *Lead me higher still,*
> *Till my life is wholly lost in Jesus*
> *And His perfect will!*   —*Jones*

THOT: When God puts a tear in your eye, it's because
He wants to put a rainbow in your heart.

SEEING GOD IN ADVERSE WINDS

*. . . and [God] was seen upon the wings
of the wind.*   2 Samuel 22:11

TWO of the world's largest cities, Chicago and
London, have suffered devastating fires. In the Chicago holocaust of 1871, more than 17,000 buildings were
burned and 250 lost their lives. In the case of London
in 1666, the damage was only about one-fifth that
much, and just four people died! What made the
London fire so much less deadly? Surprisingly, it was
a high velocity, easterly wind! One would think this
would fan the flames and increase the trouble, but instead it diminished the destruction. Here's the explanation: During the Chicago fire a great pall of smoke
hovered over the city. This layer absorbed the sun's ra-
diation and prevented the ground from cooling at
night. Many more buildings burst into flame because
of the intense heat. The only thing that could have
saved Chicago would have been a gale strong enough
to blow away that smoke—but such deliverance was
not given. In the London disaster, however, forceful
ground winds prevented the formation of a heat-
holding cover of clouds above the fire. While London-
ers at first worried about the heavy wind, it turned
out to be a great help and blessing.

So too, the "winds of adversity" in the life of the
child of God may fill him with dread; yet he eventually discovers that the Lord accomplishes His good purposes through them. Just as the people of London
shaped their plans according to the course set by the
wind, so the Christian's life is directed by the trials,
testings, and losses which plague him. He comes to
realize that God rides on the "wings of the wind" to
deliver and bless him.

> *God moves in a mysterious way*
> *His wonders to perform;*
> *He plants His footsteps in the sea*
> *And rides upon the storm!*   —Cowper

THOT: Christians should be like kites: rising highest
when the winds of adversity blow the hardest!

13

TESTED—BUT TRUSTING!

Though He slay me, yet will I trust in Him.

Job 13:15

AFTER many years of having a firm and shining testimony for God, a Christian may find himself suddenly robbed of happiness. Sorely afflicted and in dire distress—and that seemingly without rhyme or reason—he asks, "Why am I going through such terrible trials? Why do my prayers for deliverance go unanswered? Doesn't God care that I'm suffering so much?" The answer is obvious: of course He cares, but He has a wise purpose in His delays. Have you ever noticed what the Lord said to Satan about Job? God was pleased with the ancient patriarch, for Job had shown himself faithful. Often today when the Lord's people are afflicted, it's because He would exhibit them as outstanding trophies of His grace before the world and Satan. Do not disappoint the Savior, then, by being rebellious! Rather, testify with Job, "Though He slay me, yet will I trust in Him!"

A botanist described a certain vine that loves to grow alongside of oak trees. It clings to them during the fiercest storms. Even if a violent wind uproots the tree, the twining tendrils of the plant will still remain attached to it. If the vine is on the side opposite the wind, the great oak is its protection; if it is on the exposed side, the tempest only presses it closer to its host. Taking note of this, D. M. Launderville exclaims: "So in the storms of life God sometimes intervenes on our behalf and shelters us, while at other times He allows us to be exposed *so that we will be pressed more closely to Him!*"

Christian, when trials come, honor the Lord's expectation of you by praising rather than complaining!

I will commit my way, O Lord, to Thee,
Nor doubt Thy love, though dark the way may be,
Nor murmur, for the sorrow is from God,
And there is comfort also in Thy rod. —Anon.

THOT: God sends trials to IMPROVE us, not to IMPAIR us!

14

THE VALUE OF PAIN
Thou hast enlarged me when I was in distress.

Psalm 4:1

WHEN Adam fell, he died immediately in his spirit, progressively in his soul, and eventually in his body. Even though he had the sentence of death upon him, he was allowed to be the father of the human race. Thus God made possible the incarnation of Jesus Christ and the redemption of mankind. In the same progressive order, man is once again brought back to his original perfection. When we are saved, our spirits are immediately made perfect (1 John 3:9). Our souls, however, are progressively redeemed through the process of sanctification until we enter Heaven. Only there are "just men made *perfect*" (Heb. 12:23). Finally, our bodies will be touched by redemption when we are glorified in the resurrection. But in this life, Christians are subject to the same laws of sowing and reaping, pain and death that govern the physical existence of other people.

Pain is one of God's purifying agents sent to produce greater holiness in His children. Like the psalmist, they are often "enlarged" in distress. Years ago a young woman who lived in Western Canada never felt an ache or a pain. She was born without the sense of feeling! No one envied her, however, for her body often became scarred and bruised. She frequently had to be hospitalized for infections that the rest of us avoid because she didn't have the usual warning signs to alert her to danger.

The Lord often sculptures beautiful lives with the chisel of pain. So if some trial is cutting you deeply, trustingly pray, "Thank you, Lord, for this pain, and through it do Your gracious work in my life."

> *O much-tried saint with fainting heart,*
> *The thorn with its abiding pain*
> *And all its wearing, ceaseless ache*
> *Can be the means of priceless gain.* —*Anon.*

THOT: God does not afflict us to burden us, but to broaden us.

15

THE RIGHT ROAD OF AFFLICTION

Many are the afflictions of the righteous; but the Lord deliwereth him out of them all.   Psalm 34:19

SOME people think Christians who are frequently sick or in trouble are actually being punished by God for wicked deeds or unconfessed sin in their lives. But these critical assessments are frequently wide of the mark or even entirely false. Because the Lord cannot condone evil, He must at times chasten His children. Yet it is also true that the greatest saints often encounter the most severe trials. This may come as a result of their faithfulness, and it is a tribute to their holiness. Job was a "perfect man," yet God allowed Satan to test him just to prove how much he truly loved Him. The psalmist David under inspiration declared, "Many are the afflictions of the righteous."

After enduring some heartbreaking experiences, a Spirit-filled missionary was asked by a friend how he could remain so cheerful through adversity. He replied, "Suppose someone sent me on a journey and warned me that I would come first to a dangerous crossing over a river and then to a forest filled with wild beasts. I would feel a sense of satisfaction when I actually encountered these obstacles, because they would prove to me that I was traveling the right road. The same is true in the Christian life. The Lord told His disciples that they could expect tribulation. When difficulties come, therefore, I find encouragement, for I know I am walking the narrow path of God's choosing."

Afflicted one, the pathway for the righteous is often beset by thorny trials. Take courage, for they assure you that you're on *the right road Home!*

Afflictions on the good must fall,
But God will bring them safe through all;
From harmful stroke He will defend,
And sure and full deliverance send.   —Anon.

THOT: Suffering is not always sent to burn out the dross; it may be meant to burn in the promises!

16

NEEDED: FINE NEEDLEWORK

So shall the king greatly desire thy beauty; ...[when thou art clothed] in raiment of needlework. Psalm 45:11,14

IN Romans 8:18, Paul said that our sufferings "are not worthy to be compared with the glory which shall be revealed in us." When sorrows and trials are rightly received, they result in heavenly compensations. These rewards for faithful endurance far outweigh the passing pains of our earthly pilgrimage.

Commenting on this subject, Pastor Troy Corzine observed that the crushed rose gives off the sweetest fragrance, and that the pains of childbirth are compensated by the joys of motherhood. A grain of sand makes a wound in the body of an oyster, and yet from that irritation a lovely pearl is formed. Indeed, many of the beauties of Heaven will be fashioned from the bruises of earth! We should not be surprised when tribulation comes, for the psalmist tells us that the raiment we shall wear when we meet the Lord requires much intricate "needlework" here below.

It is said that Brussels lace is superior to all others because of its delicacy. The spinning is done in a pitch-black room where the light comes through one small opening and shines on the developing pattern. Some of the finest Christians live in the shadowed cubicles of bereavement and misfortune with only one light, the glow of God's love, to comfort them during the fine interlacing of His providential workings.

Weary sufferer, don't be dismayed by the needle pricks of pain and darkness. Think only of the joy of your King when you appear before Him in the fine needlework of the beauty of holiness!

My life is but a weaving between my Lord and me;
I cannot choose the colors He worketh steadily.
The dark threads are as needful in the Weaver's
  skillful hand
As the threads of gold and silver in the pattern
  He has planned. —Anon.

THOT: Trials are the raw materials out of which God weaves His miracles.

17

"IRON SAINTS"

Joseph, who was sold for a servant, whose feet they hurt with fetters; he was laid in iron.   Psalm 105:17,18

ONE commentator suggests that the last part of Psalm 105:18 might be rendered, "His soul entered into iron," or, *"Iron entered into his soul!"* As a boy, Joseph tended toward softness. He was full of dreams about his foreshadowed greatness. There may even have been a touch of pride in his makeup, for his attitude often upset his brothers. A starry-eyed idealist, he seemed to lack the strength and force of character necessary to rule. Imprisonment, however, appeared to have changed him. When he was released, he acted like a born ruler of men, displaying wisdom, modesty, courage, and firm resolution. He carried Egypt through the stress of a great famine. He held his own with the proudest aristocracy of his time, while promoting radical changes. He trusted God completely, for "iron had entered into his soul."

Friend, that's what adversity can do for us when we respond to it correctly. *God wants "iron saints"*—those who have learned patience because the binding fetters of pain have restrained their eager feet. The Lord is looking for people who have been betrayed by their dearest friends and yet have not soured under the experience. He delights to use those who have matured in the dark prison of trial and the servitude of disappointment, and have emerged triumphant by the power of grace! Yes, God imparts character and saintly attitudes in His children by letting them go through the refining furnace of trial.

Christian, are you imprisoned by difficulties? It's the Lord's way of preparing you for greater usefulness. He is infusing "iron" into your soul.

> *Afflictions, though they seem severe,*
> *Are oft in kindness sent;*
> *They fit us for God's service here,*
> *And are for blessings meant!*   —Anon.

THOT: The Lord gets His best soldiers out of the highlands of affliction!

STINGS OR HONEY?

They compassed me about like bees.

Psalm 118:12

IN the Orient, beekeepers know how to gather honey without getting stung. They wear very little protection, seldom putting a veil over their face, or donning special clothing and gloves. Yet they can be surrounded by angry bees and escape harm. The explanation is that these people are extremely deliberate in their movements. Even though a bee comes right at them, they make no effort to protect themselves. When the buzzing little creature lights on them, it makes no more attempt to sting them than it would a log or a flower. The westerner, on the other hand, is usually nervous and combative. Instead of being quiet and passive, he often runs about or waves his arms frantically. As a result, he ends up being stung.

In our psalm, the writer complains of being surrounded by enemies like one who is caught in a swarm of angry bees. Christians sometimes have similar feelings. Troubles seldom come singly; frequently they buzz around us and attack us from all points of the compass. Yet, the Oriental beekeeper gives us the key to enduring them successfully. If we fret and fume, rebelling against the trying situations of life instead of calmly trusting the Lord, we will feel the sting of defeat and miss the delightful honey of sanctification's joys. *In "quietness and confidence" is our strength!* Calm praise and trusting prayer—not frantic fretting—is the solution. Like the psalmist, we'll find that the Lord will help us if we call upon Him (Ps. 118:13).

When the "bees" of adversity engulf you, don't panic; rather, pray and praise!

Though numerous hosts of mighty foes,
Though earth and Hell my way oppose,
He safely leads my soul along,
His lovingkindness, oh, how strong!　　　　　*—Medley*

THOT: The sure cure for depression is praise!

DROPPING EVERY LEAF OF JOY

It is good for me that I have been afflicted, that
I might learn Thy statutes.   Psalm 119:71

Harriet Beecher Stowe wrote the following commentary: "It is said that gardeners, when they would bring a rose to rich flowering, deprive it for a season of light and moisture. Silent and dark it stands, dropping one faded leaf after another until it looks dead. But when the plant stands stripped to the uttermost, a new life is even then working in the buds from which shall spring a tender foliage and a brighter wealth of flowers. So, often in celestial gardenings *every leaf of earthly joy must drop before a new divine blossom visits the soul!*" I can personally testify to the truth of her words.

When I was a young boy, I contracted tuberculosis from a visiting relative. Through agonizing days and nights the disease ravaged my body. It left me physically crippled, and in some ways handicapped. Yet if I were to be given the choice of a perfectly straight, healthy body, but in exchange would have to forfeit all the blessings and sweet communion I enjoyed during those years of pain, I would never accept the offer. I might not even be saved today. Surely I would not be engaged in writing devotional meditations or be involved in many other endeavors that have eternal value. Through my trials I learned of Jesus' love, and today I have a deep, satisfying joy and peace. Yes, it has been "good for me that I have been afflicted." I shall only know *how good* when I see with the clear perspective of eternity. Praise the Lord, *He has never made a mistake in my life!* And He will lead you just as faithfully if you'll let Him.

O murmur not, Christian, He strikes but to save;
Press onward though weary—be patient and brave.
The Lord is our Refuge; and happy are they
Who hear through the whirlwind His voice and obey!

—Anon.

THOT: Learn by your reverses; you'll lose if you rebel!

LIFT YOUR EYES!

I will lift up mine eyes.

Psalm 121:1

A WOMAN who did much reading and research began to have great difficulty with her eyes and decided to consult an oculist. After an examination he said, "Madam, your eyes are just tired; you need to rest them." "But that is impossible," she replied. "My work demands that I use them almost constantly." After reflecting for a moment the doctor said, "Have you any wide views from your home?" "Oh, yes," she answered with enthusiasm, "from the front porch I can see the noble peaks of the Blue Ridge Mountains, and from the rear windows the glorious Allegheny foothills." "Very well," replied the eye doctor, "that's just what you need. When your eyes feel tired, look steadily at your mountains for 10 minutes—20 would be better—and *the far look will rest your eyes!*"

What is true in the physical is also true in the spiritual. The eyes of the soul are often weary from gazing at the problems and difficulties along the pilgrim way. With the psalmist we have to admit, "Innumerable evils have compassed me about . . . so that I am not able to look up" (Ps. 40:12). If with the Holy Spirit's help we lift our eyes *above our circumstances,* the far look will restore our perspective.

If we fail to exercise our willpower and do not set our affection on things above, God may have to take away our present treasure, dear as it may be, because it is keeping us so earthbound. In fact, He may put us on a bed of affliction to fix our gaze heavenward. May we say with spiritual determination, I will "direct my prayer unto Thee, and will look up" (Ps. 5:3).

> *I lift my eyes, though shadows cross the space*
> *That is my life, and seasons change their face,*
> *I know, come fear or war, come night or day,*
> *The hills of God shall never pass away!*   —*Zwall, alt.*

THOT: Spiritual blindness comes from failure to lift our eyes to God.

THE FIRES OF AFFLICTION

I have chosen thee in the furnace of affliction.

Isaiah 48:10

GOD is the great refiner of souls, who often passes us through the fires of affliction to purify us and to make us shine more brightly for His glory. Spurgeon said, "Comfort yourself, tried believer, with this thought in Isaiah 48:10. Let affliction come—God has chosen me. Sickness may intrude, but I have a balm ready—God has chosen me. Whatever befalls me in this fiery trial, I know the Lord permitted it because He has set His love upon me. Believer, if you require still greater comfort, remember that you have the Son of man with you in the furnace! In that silent chamber of yours, One whom you love sits by your side who will make your bed in your affliction and smooth your pillow. He said, 'Fear thou not; for I am with thee. Be not dismayed; for I am thy God.' His presence is both your comfort and safety." Yes, the Lord often selects His "spiritual statesmen" in the flames of trial and opposition. In the furnace of sevenfold heat the refining process removes their dross.

If you have asked the Savior to use you as a witness to His grace, don't think it strange when He sends a fiery trial to prepare you for such a noble endeavor. The three friends of Daniel in Nebuchadnezzar's furnace were not hurt by its flames. *They lost only their bonds!* Emerging from their ordeal as "heroes of faith," they brought glory to God and were promoted to higher service (Dan. 3:28-30).

In your present difficult circumstances you too can find many God-given opportunities. Remember, the Lord chooses His best workers in the furnace of affliction.

When through fiery trials thy pathway shall lie,
My grace all-sufficient shall be thy supply;
The flame shall not hurt thee—I only design
Thy dross to consume, and thy gold to refine.   —*Anon.*

THOT: Fires of suffering produce tempered saints.

PRECIOUS JEWELS

And they shall be Mine, saith the Lord . . . ,
when I make up My jewels.   Malachi 3:17

SOMEDAY the Lord will return from Heaven to collect His "jewels" so that they may shine eternally in the kingdom of His Father (Dan. 12:3; Mt. 13:43). In this life God often puts us upon the grinding wheel of affliction that He may begin the buffeting process His "rough gems" require. If we will just remember that these unpleasant experiences are adding to our "preciousness," we will take the abrasiveness of adversity with joy and unwavering faithfulness.

"While in Amsterdam, Holland, last summer," said a traveler, "I was very much interested in a visit we made to a place that was famous for polishing diamonds. We saw many men engaged in the work. When a diamond is found, it is rough and dark like a common pebble. It takes many long hard hours to polish it. The stone is held against the surface of a large revolving wheel. Fine diamond dust is used as a grinding powder, for nothing else is hard enough to polish it. The buffing continues for months. If the diamond is intended for some dignitary, then even more time must be spent on it."

The Lord's saved children are called His "jewels." To be prepared for beautifying His crown, we must be polished like diamonds. He therefore allows trouble to buffet us, that we may lose our inner darkness and more clearly reflect His glory. To acquire the many-sided bevel of holiness, sin and evil habits must be ground from our character.

Are you one of His "precious jewels"? Then do not be surprised if in this life you get a "good polishing"!

> *Like the stars of the morning,*
> *His bright crown adorning,*
> *They shall shine in their beauty—*
> *Bright gems for His crown!*   —Cushing

THOT: God's jewels are gathered in grace, polished by pain, and destined for His diadem!

23

THE BAROMETER OF BLESSING

Blessed are ye, when men shall hate you . . .
for the Son of man's sake.   Luke 6:22

IF you are encountering opposition as a child of God, it may well indicate that you are doing something that really counts for eternity. When Paul and his helpers persuaded the people of Ephesus that they should worship Christ rather than the goddess Diana, the silversmiths who made images of her became angry and incited a riot. The Lord knows that those who do His work will incur the hatred of sinful men. So, when He forewarned His followers that they would face persecution, He also encouraged them to go forward in spite of the bitter attacks of the enemy (John 16:33).

For more than 21 years, Edward Vander Jagt and I conducted outdoor gospel meetings during the summer months. When a man who had been a member of a false cult accepted Christ, we soon began to experience the opposition of Satan. As backsliders were reclaimed and conversions became more frequent, the trouble increased and even took the form of violence. Our expensive sound system was stolen, the enclosed platform area was forcibly entered, and the piano was chopped to pieces. Obscenities were painted on the building, powerlines were cut, and motorcycle gangs disturbed the quiet of the services. Yet we never missed a meeting. Wanting to obey our Lord, we did not complain but rejoiced instead. We knew that the devil was angry because God's work was prospering.

Believer, if you are being persecuted for righteousness' sake, be encouraged. *It's a barometer of the Lord's blessing!* Never lose faith. "If God be for us, who can be against us?" (Rom. 8:31).

Forbid it, Lord, that I should be
  Afraid of persecution's frown;
For Thou hast promised faithful ones
  That they shall wear the victor's crown.   —Bosch

THOT: Work for the Lord—the pay isn't much but the retirement plan is "out of this world."

HAMMER BLOWS OF AFFLICTION

*... we must through much tribulation enter
into the kingdom of God.*   Acts 14:22

TO conform us to the image of His dear Son, our Heavenly Father often subjects us to "much tribulation." Someone has written: "There are unsculptured figures in the quarries of life which only the blasts of misfortune and the chisels of adversity can carve into beauty." The words of the poet agree: "When God wants to mold a man/ To play the noblest part,/ When He yearns with all His heart/ To create so bold a man/ That the world will be amazed,/ Watch His methods, watch His ways./ How He ruthlessly perfects/ Whom He royally elects!/ How He hurts and hammers him,/ With mighty blows converts him/ Into trial shapes of clay/ Which He only understands."

A. T. Pierson told of watching a blacksmith working at his trade. With a small hammer the smithy touched the white-hot iron on the anvil and nodded to his helper to hit as hard as he could with a heavy sledge. The minister asked, "Why do you first dent it with such tiny taps?" "Oh, I'm just showing him where to hit," was the reply. Dr. Pierson thought for a moment and then said, "I think we can draw a parable from your actions. Often God puts His finger on the weak points in His servant's life or work, and then permits the devil to bring down the sledgehammer blows of affliction to forge him into a stronger man and a better Christian. Thus He makes the devil sweat for the saint's benefit!"

As a believer, are you enduring many trials? If so, rejoice that God has honored you to suffer for His sake, for great will be your reward in Heaven.

> *For every pain that we must bear,*
>   *For every sorrow, every care—there is a reason;*
> *But if we trust Him as we should,*
>   *All things will work out for our good—God knows*
>   *the reason!*   —Anon.

THOT: Where saints are being tried and tested, there God is hewing out pillars for His temple.

WHEN ALL IS "CHOCOLATE CAKE"

*And we know that all things work together for
good to them that love God.*   Romans 8:28

THE believer in Christ is faced with many situations in life that are not actually good in themselves. Yet the Lord promises to transform these trying circumstances into heavenly blessings that will far outweigh the problems they caused us.

Wendell P. Loveless gave a helpful illustration of this truth. Speaking of Romans 8:28, he said, "My wife can make better chocolate cake than anyone I know. So one day I thought I'd go into the kitchen and see what wonderful ingredients she used. First she sifted some flour—this didn't appeal to me at all, for it was dry and unappetizing. Next she added a cup of sour milk. Now the batter looked very distasteful. Then, to make matters worse, she put in a raw egg. By this time I was not too sure whether I liked chocolate cake or not. I left just as she was popping it into the oven. Much to my surprise, that evening her masterpiece was as delicious as any she ever baked! This is the spiritual lesson I learned: Often in life we encounter 'dry stretches' which are tasteless and uninviting like the flour. We also meet with 'sour' experiences like the milk, and even a few 'raw deals' like the egg; but after we have gone through the oven of affliction, praise God, all will become a sweet and flavorful blessing over There!"

Dear one in Christ, don't fret when troubles come! God is "mixing the batter" of your life according to a marvelous recipe. After the heat of earth's trials will come the rewarding "dessert" of Heaven. Then—speaking reverently—all will be "chocolate cake"!

> *God works together all our woe*
> *And brightens with His love;*
> *The trials that we suffer here*
> *Bring rich rewards above.*   —Anon.

THOT: If you're taking a beating, cheer up; God is just stirring the batter to bring you a blessing.

GETTING IN SHAPE

For which cause we faint not; ... though our outward man perish.   2 Corinthians 4:16

AN evangelist was quoted in an English publication as having told the following true story in one of his campaigns: "I have a friend who lost a job, a fortune, a wife, and a home during the depression but tenaciously held to his faith—the only thing he had left. One day he stopped to watch some men doing stonework on a huge church. Seeing a master craftsman chiseling a triangular piece of rock, he asked, 'What are you going to do with that?' The workman said, 'Do you see that little opening way up there near the spire? Well, *I am shaping this down here so that it will fit in up there.*' Tears filled my friend's eyes as he walked away, for it seemed that God had spoken through that stonemason to explain the ordeal through which he was passing."

You may also be going through difficult times. Perhaps you are experiencing much pain and physical disability. The outward man seems to be "perishing." Yet, if you are a child of God, you should not despair nor "faint"; for all these things are from the loving hand of your Father. He is getting you in shape for the heavenly mansions.

All of us live in bodies of clay which will soon return to the dust. But as God molds the pliable putty of our human frailty, He makes possible for us a "far more exceeding and eternal weight of glory" (2 Cor. 4:17). These heavenly rewards will be ours if our inward man is shaped through the process to conform more perfectly to His divine will.

The chisel of trial may hurt, but remember, it is "shaping you down here so you will fit in up There!"

> Be this the purpose of my soul,
> My solemn, my determined choice,
> To yield to Thy supreme control,
> And in my every trial rejoice.   —Anon.

THOT: However dark the "now" may be, there will be light enough in God's "after" to explain it all.

27

THE CUTS MAKE THE DIFFERENCE

For our light affliction ... worketh for us a far more
exceeding and eternal weight of glory.   2 Corinthians 4:17

GOD calls His children "jewels" (Mal. 3:17), and
jewels need to be skillfully cut by a master craftsman
if all their latent beauty is to be revealed. This truth
led a French pastor to comfort an afflicted woman
with these words: "Dear sister in Christ, notice that I
hold in my hand two stones. They are alike in color
and are equally pure. Yet there's a marked contrast
between them. One has a dazzling brilliance; the
other is quite dull." "What makes the difference?" inquired the woman. "Any dealer in precious stones
could give you the answer," said her pastor. "It's because *one has received 80 cuts from the jeweler's chisel,
and the other only 8.* The stone that has 'suffered
much' is radiant, but the one that has had little effort
expended on it is dim and lusterless." He then reminded the lady that her light affliction, which was only
temporary, was working for her an "eternal weight of
glory." He told her she should therefore accept her
trials with joy, because they were not worthy to be
compared with the reward she would eventually receive when she would stand before the Lord.

Yes, the hammer blows of suffering and pain are designed by the Master to shape us into objects of spiritual beauty and worth. Because of His divine "chiseling," we will soon begin to shine with His reflected
glory. The results will be manifested not only now but
throughout the eternal ages (Dan. 12:3).

Have you seen a life aglow for God? Investigation
will probably show that the cuts of trial have made
the sparkling difference.

> *Whenever my trials seem heavy*
>   *And burdens are pressing me sore,*
> *I know that the Master is busy*
>   *Perfecting His precious stone more.*   —*Anon.*

THOT: Troubles are not sent to batter us but to
    better us.

THE GIFT OF A THORN

And lest I should be exalted above measure . . ., there was given to me a thorn in the flesh. 2 Corinthians 12:7

WHAT a strange gift Paul was given—a sharp, irritating thorn! But it accomplished God's purpose by reminding the apostle that he was just a weak man. It *hindered* him, but it also *humbled* him. Whatever this affliction was, it contributed greatly to his sanctification, for he wrote, "Most gladly, therefore will I rather glory in my infirmities, that the power of Christ may rest upon me" (2 Cor. 12:9).

Our trials too can be cause for rejoicing if we view them properly. Such experiences are very painful to the flesh, and our first reaction is to avoid them. But if we accept them as coming from God's gracious hand, they will prove to be a blessing. Such thorns are inevitably attached to the roses of grace whose eternal fragrance will make our lives attractive to others.

In the words of George Matheson may we humbly pray, "My God, I have never thanked Thee for my thorn. I have thanked Thee a thousand times for my roses, but not once for my thorn. I have been looking forward to a world where I should get compensation for my crosses, but I have never thought of my cross as itself a present glory. Thou, Divine Love, whose human path has been perfected through sufferings, teach me the value of my thorn, . . . and then shall I know that my tears have made my rainbow, and I shall be able to say, it is good for me that I have been afflicted."

If you are experiencing trials, accept them as coming from the Heavenly Father. Remember, some of the most beautiful roses are found among the sharpest thorns.

> *Then murmur not if toils obscure*
> *And thorny paths be thine;*
> *To God be true—they shall secure*
> *The joy of life divine.* —Anon.

THOT: God can weave the thorns of life into a crown of glory.

ING ABOVE THE CIRCUMSTANCES

he things which happened unto me have fallen out rather unto the furtherance of the gospel.   Philippians 1:12

BY grace the apostle Paul was able to view his hardship and imprisonment in the light of eternity. Therefore, when circumstances or his enemies seemed to hinder his ministry, he rejoiced that despite outward appearances all things were actually working for his good and "the furtherance of the gospel."

A friend of mine once met a lady who was severely depressed by a series of disheartening events. When asked how she was doing, she answered, "Quite well, under the circumstances!" "Sister," he replied firmly, "you'll never make it that way. Get ABOVE the circumstances—that's where Jesus waits to help and strengthen you!" She took his wise admonition as a word from Heaven. Laying aside her sadness and self-pity, she began to praise the Lord. New confidence in God's love and kindness was generated in her soul, and soon she gained the victory of faith.

An unknown poet wrote these comments on today's Scripture: "Circumstances! How we pet them; how we give them right of way!/ But the Master never planned that we should fall beneath their sway./ Paul made circumstances serve him, made them glorify his Lord;/ Turned each trial into blessing as he boldly preached the Word./ 'These things turned to my advantage,' this old warrior oft would say;/ 'For our good they work together,' though they seem to shroud the day."

Don't let the shadows of earth darken your testimony, Christian. Faith and praise are two unfailing antidotes for gloom and self-pity. You'll never find peace unless you learn to live "ABOVE the circumstances"!

Lord, I would clasp Thy hand in mine,
Nor ever murmur nor repine;
Content, whatever lot I see,
Since 'tis my God that leadeth me!   —Gilmore

THOT: Never despair—man's extremity is God's opportunity.

ONE THUMB—BUT THANKFUL!

In everything give thanks.   1 Thessalonians 5:18
. . . godliness with contentment is great gain.   1 Timothy 6:6

THE noted Bible teacher Wendell P. Loveless once wrote: "I want to share with you the story of a friend of mine who lives in Illinois. She is a 64-year-old woman who has been shut in for more than 16 years. Confined to her bed and in constant pain, she is unable to move a limb. But listen! She's one of the most thankful people I've ever met. She rejoices that God has left her a great blessing—the use of the thumb of her right hand! The other hand is clenched and stiff and utterly useless. With a two-pronged fork fastened to a stick she can put on her glasses and remove them again, but all with great effort. By the same method she can feed herself and sip her tea through a tube. She does all this, using only her one thumb. She can also turn the leaves of a large Bible when it is placed within her reach. A visitor once heard her say joyfully, 'I have so much to be thankful for.' When she was asked the source of this happiness, she answered, 'Now that my sins are all forgiven, I can just lay back and daily drink in the great love of Jesus my Savior.' Her restricted way of life did not make her fretful and despondent, for she said, 'I'm perfectly content to lie here as long as it pleases the Lord to let me stay in this world, and I'm also ready to leave whenever He calls me.'"

Perhaps you too are confined by illness or infirmity, but that's no excuse to grumble and complain. Remember the courage shown by this severely handicapped lady and follow her spiritual example. Be truly grateful for the opportunities and abilities God still grants to you—and rejoice!

> When I think how much He's blessed me,
>   All life's trials lose their sting;
> I am thankful for His mercies,
>   And my heart begins to sing.   —Anon.

THOT: The praise-life will give you victory over the self-life.

"THE HARDNESS OF GOD'S LOVE"

For whom the Lord loveth He chasteneth, and scourgeth every son whom He receiveth. Hebrews 12:6

ON one of his field trips a Christian biology student found the large, flask-shaped cocoon of an emperor moth. Intrigued by its peculiar construction, he decided to watch how the full-grown insect would eventually be able to force its way out of the narrow opening on one end. He didn't realize that the pressure the insect's body is subjected to in passing through such a small "escape hatch" is essential. It's a provision planned by God to force the juices into the vessels of the moth's wings. Sometime later the young man noticed that the insect was trying to emerge from its cocoon but never seemed to get beyond a certain point. At last his patience was exhausted, so he took a scissors and clipped a few of the confining threads around the opening. Immediately and with perfect ease the moth emerged, but it dragged behind its huge swollen body some badly shriveled wings. The man's tenderness in helping the creature became its ruin. It never was anything but a stunted abortion, bloated and ugly, when it should have spent hours flying through the air on rainbow wings. The student of biology said, "That taught me a lesson. I came to understand the deep meaning of the phrase '*the hardness of God's love.*' I've thought of it often when watching someone struggling with suffering and distress. It seemed to me that I would be more merciful and give them deliverance. Shortsighted fool! The divine love that seeks to perfect us does not shrink from allowing us transient trouble, because He truly cares for His own!"

God permits suffering to sanctify us and bring us rich rewards.

> *Oh, I have found 'tis good for me*
> *To bear my Father's rod;*
> *Affliction makes me learn His will,*
> *And lean upon my God.*   —Anon.

THOT: Have patience—crowns are cast out of crucibles.

32

CONSIDER HIM AND
STOP WRIGGLING!

*For consider Him ... lest ye be wearied and faint
in your minds.*   Hebrews 12:3

OUR precious Savior endured shame, contradiction of sinners, and extreme suffering and pain—oblivious of what it cost Him personally—so that He might do the Father's will. In all of this He set us a blessed example. We are encouraged to face the trials of life with enduring faith and unwavering good cheer. When we undergo troubles and difficulties, we are not to view them as something sent by God to injure us. Rather, it's His invitation to call upon His higher resources for special grace to endure them. In that way our soul will be enriched with new and fragrant blessings.

A Christian worker had been treated most unkindly and was crying brokenheartedly when a neighbor came in, laid a hand on her shoulder, and said, *"I'm sorry to see you wriggling!"* "What do you mean?" the woman asked. "Well," said the neighbor, "when a goldsmith puts his precious metal into the crucible and the fire begins to work on the dross, it wriggles and writhes. But as the impurity is burned out it quiets down and becomes more placid. At last the surface is so calm that the *refiner can see his own face reflected!* He knows then that he can put out the fire, for the gold is pure. When I saw you crying because of the flame of trial and persecution, I realized that instead of rejoicing in His will and thus reflecting the Savior, you were still wriggling!"

Tried one, consider Christ. Stop your wriggling and your gold will be refined. God will then be able to put out "the fire."

When sorrows assail us or terrors draw nigh,
His love will not fail us, He'll guard with His eye;
And when we are fainting and ready to fail,
He'll give what is wanting and make us prevail.   —Anon.

THOT: Let Him fill your vision, and all else will be
       crowded out.

COUNT IT ALL JOY!

My brethren, count it all joy when ye fall into
various trials.   James 1:2

A NURSE in a servicemen's hospital went to the chaplain and complained that she was being treated rudely by some of the patients. He answered, "Thank God for that!" "What do you mean?" she inquired in astonishment. "Well," he explained, "if you're holding a glass and someone knocks against you, you can only spill out what is inside! If people misjudge us or persecute us, we soon reveal what is in our hearts. If we are Christ-filled and governed by the Holy Spirit, we will manifest the gentleness and meekness of our Savior. God often allows us to be pushed around and jostled so that the unsaved may be astonished at His grace as we overflow with love and forbearance."

Often our troubles and testings seem depressing and cruel, but James, under divine inspiration, told us to count them all joy. Knowing that God perfectly directs our lives, we should praise Him rather than complain. *Difficulties then become opportunities!* Gracious restraint and humble self-denial are attitudes that glorify Jesus. Paul says, "Being reviled, we bless; being persecuted, we endure it; being defamed, we entreat" (1 Cor. 4:12,13).

Commentators say that John Bunyan was such an earnest and devoted Christian that he actually asked the Lord to send cruel mockings and severe trials to give him new opportunities to show his love for Jesus. He thoroughly delighted in displaying God's grace.

Are you irritated, grumpy, and full of complaints when the going gets rough? Or do you welcome these experiences as a challenge and "count it all joy"?

I used to doubt the love of God who let me suffer so,
And in despair and agony the bitter tears would flow;
I now no longer ask for things, for Christ is my desire;
He walks with me and talks with me, He is my Satisfier!

                                                                —Bang

THOT: If we have Jesus on the inside, we can stand
           any kind of trouble on the outside!

34

THE MILL OF TRIAL

That the trial of your faith ... might be found unto praise ...
and glory at the appearing of Jesus Christ. 1 Peter 1:7

MANY trials cross the Christian's pathway. To compensate for them, there is "joy unspeakable and full of glory" if the believer is sanctified through them. A. T. Pierson illustrated this truth as follows: "Once I had the privilege of watching pulp and rags being made into paper. What a contrast there was between the heap of filthy rags at one end of the process and the pure, spotless, white paper at the other! What a trial the rags go through before they emerge in this new form! Torn to pieces and ground to pulp, bleached with chloride of lime till all stains are removed, washed over and over, submitted to another bleaching by the action of chlorine and alum; washed again, till the pulp is white as cream or snowflakes! Caught upon a wire cylinder, it is then shaken until the fibers are crossed. This gives compactness and firmness to the fabric. Next it is passed between and around the hot surfaces which make the paper smooth and even. How like the Divine discipline by which our filthiness is cleansed away! How like the tribulation out of which all come who have washed their robes in the blood of the Lamb!"

The Bible is full of stories about God's children who have "gone through the mill." Note the afflicted Job on the ash heap, lonely Daniel in the lion's den, exiled John on the isle of Patmos, thorn-troubled Paul, and the many unnamed martyrs in Hebrews 11.

Believer, if you are suffering, you are in excellent company—the company of the heroes of faith whose trials, like yours, will one day be richly rewarded.

Should Thy mercy send me sorrow, toil, and woe,
Or should pain attend me on my path below,
Grant that I may never fail Thy hand to see;
Grant that I may ever cast my care on Thee.

— *Montgomery*

THOT: Afflictions are often God's best blessings sent in disguise.

35

2. Burdens

As a general rule, Christians in this world are subjected to many heavy trials. Paul speaks of this truth in 2 Corinthians 5:4. He declares that we who "are in this tabernacle do groan, being burdened." Yet we should not despair, for if rightly received, they can bring us many blessings.

I am told that when people in Africa must pass through rushing waters they frequently place a weight upon their heads. They say this gives them surefootedness as they walk along the unknown bottom of a stream. The Lord uses the same principle with us, His children. He puts a burden upon our hearts, not to crush us, but to keep us from slipping on the steep hills of difficulty. The load we carry will give us traction as we tread the winding path that leads to the spiritual mountaintop of victory.

Admittedly, we must endure most adverse experiences alone. We cannot shift these weights of woe to the backs of others. Yet we may be sure that our Lord never lays an unreasonable burden upon us. Although the pressure may at first seem unbearable, it will grow surprisingly lighter as we ascend the heights of sanctification.

At other times we can in part roll our burden upon the Lord, and He will help us bear them. This will ease our heavy load of care and comfort our spirit.

An anonymous poet has written this perceptive bit of verse:

"The road is too rough," I said. "Dear Lord,
   There are stones that hurt me so."
And He said, "Dear child, I understand;
   I walked it long ago."

"But there's a cool green path," I said;
   "Let me walk there for a time."
"No, child," He gently answered me,
   "The green road does not climb."

"My burden," I said, "is far too great;
   How can I bear it so?"
"My child," said He, "I remember its weight;
   I carried My cross, you know."

And so I climbed the stony path,
   Content at last to know
That where my Master had not gone
   I would not need to go.

Never forget: burdens borne in faith become blessings!

"WHAT HE HAS GIVEN THEE"

*Cast thy burden upon the Lord, and He
shall sustain thee.*   Psalm 55:22

THE Hebrew word for "burden" in this text, which is used only once in the entire Old Testament, literally means, *"what He has given thee."* Because we worry needlessly, we take unnecessary cares upon ourselves. But the Lord did not promise to bear these anxieties for us. Yet He's always ready to help us through any trial that comes from His gracious hand.

A believer who had many problems of his own dreamed that he saw a multitude of men and women who were weighed down with various burdens. Although all the people were Christians, each was staggering beneath a heavy load. He was amazed to see that from time to time the Lord Himself permitted their oppression to increase. Still the weary ones went on, though they were almost ready to drop in their tracks from exhaustion. To add to their grief, even more afflictions were piled upon them. The dreamer, greatly perplexed, humbly approached the Lord and asked why He allowed this to happen. The Savior replied, "I'm letting their distress build up until they can no longer do without My help. Then, as they turn to Me in desperation, I'll carry both them and their burdens." The Christian awoke with a start. Suddenly he realized that instead of questioning God's goodness and help in his own trials, he should have brought his weighty problems to the One who is the great burden-bearer and mighty comforter.

The apostle Peter reiterated the advice of the psalmist to cast our care upon the Lord, giving this word of assurance, "He careth for you" (1 Pet. 5:7).

Christ will not fail me, a child of His care;
All of my burdens He gladly will share.
With Him beside me, ill cannot harm me;
When I most need Him, my Lord will be there.

—Poole, alt.

THOT: Our work is to CAST CARE; God's work is to
        TAKE CARE!

GOD KNOWS WHAT WE CAN CARRY

For He knoweth our frame; He remembereth
that we are dust.   Psalm 103:14

GOD is tenderly concerned about our frailties. He made us, and He knows our innate weaknesses. As a father pities his children, so the Lord cares for us when we are overwhelmed by adversity. If we prayerfully look to Him in our troubles, He will not allow our burdens to become greater than we can bear.

A man was shopping in a grocery store with his small son following closely behind him. The boy was carrying a large basket, and the father loaded it with one item after another. He put in canned goods, sugar, flour, meat, and a variety of vegetables. A customer watching nearby began to feel sorry for the struggling youngster. Walking up behind him, she said quietly, "That's a heavy load for a little chap like you to carry, isn't it?" The boy turned to her as if surprised that anyone needed to be told. Then he smiled confidently and said, "Oh, don't worry, *my dad knows how much I can carry!*"

Our Heavenly Father knows the limit of our endurance. He understands precisely how much we can take. He is too kind to do anything to hurt us, and He is too wise to make any mistakes. Therefore, no Christian can truthfully say about his trials, "They are too much for me." Frances Ridley Havergal, the hymnwriter, has given us this reminder:

"As thy days thy strength shall be!"
This should be enough for thee;
He who knows thy frame will spare
Burdens more than thou canst bear.

Cheer up, Christian, God knows how much you can carry!

> *We should not question trials sore*
> *Or sorrows hard to bear,*
> *But look in love to Him above*
> *Who wisely placed them there.* —*Adams, alt.*

THOT: The God who knows our "load limit" graciously limits our load.

AN ELM OR AN EVERGREEN?

I am like a green fir tree. From me is thy fruit found.

Hosea 14:8

THE *Wall Street Journal* once carried the story of a youngster named Sally who was so conscientious that she made herself miserable over minor tragedies. Early one fall after an exceptionally heavy snowstorm, her grandfather took her for a drive. "Notice those elms," he said. "The branches are so badly broken that the trees may die. But look at the pines and evergreens—they are undamaged by the storm. My child, there are only two kinds of trees in the world: the stubborn and the wise. An elm holds its branches rigid, and when the weight becomes too heavy, its limbs finally break—disfiguring or killing it. But when an evergreen is loaded with more than it can hold, it simply lowers its branches and lets the burden slip away, remaining unharmed. Be a pine tree, granddaughter. Bear what you can, and let the rest of the load slide off."

In checking, I found that the first time the Bible mentions the pine is in 2 Samuel 6:5, "David and all the house of Israel played before the Lord on . . . instruments made of fir wood." This tree is also associated with building the temple (1 Ki. 5:10; Isa. 60:13). Some Bible teachers believe that the first time a thing is mentioned in Scripture it displays certain characteristics which cling to it throughout the Word. Applying this rule, the fir tree is associated with praise and sanctification.

Are you like the elm that tries to bear all its own burdens, only to be broken in the process? Or are you like the "green fir tree," praising God in your trials and allowing the main burden to "slide off" on Him?

> *By casting all your care on Jesus*
> *You'll find relief from grief and pain;*
> *For He will lift the load that's pressing*
> *And give to you a song again!*   —Bosch

THOT: God tells us to burden Him with whatever burdens us.

TELLING JESUS

And his disciples came ... and told Jesus.

Matthew 14:12

JOHN the Baptist had just been beheaded by the wicked Herod because of his witness for Christ, and his disciples were greatly saddened and upset. Lovingly they buried the body of their zealous leader. Then, because such a tragic sorrow must find an outlet somewhere, they turned to the most interested party and the most sympathetic ear—they went and told Jesus! Christians today must constantly be reminded that the very best thing they can possibly do with every need, burden, and perplexity is to go quickly to the Savior and tell Him about it. The poet said: "In thy weakness, in thy peril,/ Raise to Him a heartfelt call;/ Strength and calm for every crisis/ Comes in telling Jesus all."

When I was a child, a Christian neighbor who lived down the street experienced a great sorrow. She had often played and sung at her piano, but after that tragedy she would always begin her "daily concert" with the lovely hymn "I Must Tell Jesus." The words made a deep impression upon me as a child: "I must tell Jesus all of my troubles,/ He is a kind, compassionate Friend;/ If I but ask Him, He will deliver,/ Make of my troubles quickly an end./ I must tell Jesus! I must tell Jesus!/ I cannot bear these burdens alone;/ I must tell Jesus! I must tell Jesus!/ Jesus can help me, Jesus alone." I learned afterward that she not only found grace in her time of need, but God gave her such a marvelous answer to her prayers that her burden became a blessing.

Are problems pressing in on you from every side? Are you heavyhearted? TELL IT TO JESUS!

> *Are you weary, are you heavyhearted?*
> *Tell it to Jesus, tell it to Jesus;*
> *Are you grieving over joys departed?*
> *Tell it to Jesus alone.* —Rankin

THOT: There is no place where earth's sorrows are more keenly felt than in Heaven.

41

WHAT TO DO WITH BURDENS

And take heed to yourselves, lest at any time your hearts
be overcharged with ... cares of this life.   Luke 21:34

WHEN cares weigh heavily upon us, we have a
tendency to let them divert us from our sacred duties
and obligations. Jesus warns us of the danger of
becoming so overloaded with earthly concerns that we
lose perspective and no longer live for His glory.

Isaac Page told the story of a man in Ireland who
was too poor to own any type of transportation. One
day he was plodding along toward home, carrying
such a huge bag of potatoes that from time to time his
knees buckled. A man with a horse and wagon finally
caught up with him on the road, and the driver
stopped and invited him to climb aboard. The overloaded man immediately accepted, but when he sat
down he continued to hold the heavy bag of potatoes
in his arms. When the driver suggested that he should
set his load down on the floor of the wagon, he replied
very warmly in his Irish brogue, "Sure and I don't like
to trouble you too much, sir. You're a givin' me a ride
already, so I'll just carry the potatoes." How foolish!
we say. Yet sometimes we do the same when we attempt to bear in our own strength the distressing
burdens of the hour. No wonder we become so weary
that we nearly collapse! How much better to place
upon the Lord that which He offers to carry, and so
find sweet rest in His sustaining grace!

When you recall the incident of this misguided
Irishman, think as well of the simple lesson it illus-
trates. Most of our burdens can be placed in the wagon
of God's sure help. So don't try to carry your cumber-
some load in your own strength.

> *Upon the Lord your burden cast,*
> *To Him bring all your care;*
> *He will sustain and hold you fast,*
> *And give you strength to bear.*   —*Anon.*

THOT: When you struggle to carry your own burden,
you rule out the strength of the Lord.

CHEERFUL IN TRIBULATION

In the world ye shall have tribulation: but be of
good cheer; I have overcome the world.   John 16:33

THE apostle Paul recognized that many of life's most valuable lessons are spelled out with tears. Although he had been beaten, stoned, and severely afflicted, he steadfastly followed the Lord and continued to be of "good cheer." In keeping with the teachings of Jesus, the apostle told Christians to rejoice and "give thanks" (1 Th. 5:18), even in trials.

Years ago a small group of Japanese believers were heckled and abused whenever they assembled to worship the Savior. But the persecutors could not shake the faith of the new converts. Each time they gathered, the mob would throw stones at them, but they still faithfully continued to have their weekly meetings. Eventually the opposition became so great that the outdoor services had to be abandoned. Later, when a time of peace and tolerance had come to the community, many of its citizens were won to Christ. A group of the converts returned to the spot where they had been frequently attacked and began to pick up some of the rocks. Using them as building materials, they constructed a small house of worship, and rejoiced that God had worked all things together for good.

Jesus said that His followers would meet with suffering and heartache, but He admonished them not to be discouraged. Earth's sorrows are meant to be steppingstones in the process of sanctification. Indeed, we "must through much tribulation enter into the kingdom of God" (Acts 14:22). If we glory in our affliction, we'll turn our troubles and burdens into spiritual triumphs.

> *Do burdens press? Still be content, poor heart;*
>   *God's plans like lilies purest white unfold.*
> *We must not tear the close-shut leaves apart;*
>   *Time will reveal the calyxes of gold.*   —Anon.

THOT: As storms develop strong trees, so burdens make strong Christians.

TETHERED BY ADVERSITY

And we know that all things work together for good
to them that love God.   Romans 8:28

CHRISTIAN friend, are you passing through a time of trial and disappointment? Are you shackled by circumstances that seem to slow your progress and quench your zeal? Don't fret! God has a wise purpose in allowing those obstructing events to come your way.

A gentleman in England was visiting a friend who had a stable of famous riding horses. He noticed that one of the beautiful animals feeding in the pasture had a weight fastened to its leg, which hindered its free motion. "Why did you put a clog on that fine horse?" he asked. His friend replied, "I'd much rather do that than let him run free. He has a tendency to leap over fences and hedges, and he could permanently injure himself if he were not controlled." The owner was using good judgment, even though the animal didn't like being restrained. So too, God sometimes puts a tether on our lives to keep us from endangering ourselves and others.

J. B. Nicholson made this helpful comment: "Many a tried and perplexed child of God has cried out, 'What good can ever come out of this?'" Well, the "good" of Romans 8:28 is answered in part by the "glory" of verse 29, which tells us that by these things we are being conformed to the image of God's Son. Someday the Lord will finish the work He has already begun here through those restraining circumstances and the discipline of His perfect will.

Yes, child of God, the tether of adversity is meant to keep you in the place of safety and blessing. Eternity will reveal that all of life's obstacles which hinder and distress you are working together for your good.

> *You may know beyond all doubting*
> *In this trial you're passing through*
> *That a loving God sustains you,*
> *And some good He's planned for you.*   —Anon.

THOT: No trial would trouble you if you knew God's purpose in sending it.

44

THE BLESSING OF BURDENS

*I [will] rather glory in my infirmities, that the power
of Christ may rest upon me.*   2 Corinthians 12:9

THE life of the apostle Paul gives us a blessed example of patient suffering. In the face of crushing conditions, he exclaimed, "I take pleasure in infirmities, in reproaches, in necessities, in persecutions, in distresses for Christ's sake; for when I am weak, then am I strong" (2 Cor. 12:10). As Christians, we have no right to fall into spiritual defeat beneath the load laid upon us, crushing though it may seem to be. Our trials ought to make us rejoice. God is making us weak so that He may bestow upon us the power of Christ. He would teach us not to glory in our own insignificant vitality, but rather in His almighty, never-failing strength!

An old grandfather clock had stood for three generations in the same corner, faithfully ticking off the minutes, hours, and days. A heavy weight inside was pulled to the top each night to keep the clock running. "Too bad," thought the new owner, "that such an old clock should have to bear so great a load." So he took the heavy weight off the hook and removed it from the clock. At once the old clock stopped ticking. "Why did you do that?" asked the clock. "I wanted to lighten your burden," said the man. "Please," said the clock, "put it back. That is what keeps me going!"

Too many are looking for an easy way through life. They think that if they had no burdens they could live pleasantly and triumphantly. They don't realize that God often keeps us up spiritually by keeping us down physically! If they are rightly received, our burdens will work for us an exceeding and eternal weight of reward (2 Cor. 4:17).

One day at a time, and the day is His day;
He hath numbered its hours, though they haste or delay,
His grace is sufficient; we walk not alone;
As the day, so the strength that He giveth His own! —Flint

THOT: The burden you are feeling is only the weight
of the Potter's hand forming you for His glory.

45

BURDENS OR WINGS?

For every man shall bear his own burden.

Galatians 6:5

AN ancient legend gives a fanciful description of the creation of the birds. They were given sweet voices and colorful plumage, but at first were not equipped for flying. Then they saw some beautiful wings lying on the ground. When they were told to take these burdens and bear them, the birds replied, "Burdens? Oh, how dreadful! But we will carry them as bravely and cheerfully as we can." So, although they dreaded to do so, they carried them along. Then something wonderful happened! The burdens began to grow and attach themselves to their bodies. The feathered creatures stretched them out and suddenly found that with them they were able to fly. What had been called burdens were really lovely pinions. The birds would never have been able to soar gracefully into the clear, blue heavens without them. The story is pure fiction, but it does teach a worthwhile lesson: Our burdens also can be turned into wings that will bring us spiritual blessings! If we take them to our hearts with liberal amounts of grace, they'll bear us nearer to God and Heaven.

In life we have burdens of physical pain, heartache, and soul distress that others cannot bear for us, though they want to help us. These disagreeable things may seem unbearable; yet the Lord will never give us more than we can carry. In fact, these difficulties are sent to help us ascend to new heights of sanctification as we stretch our wings of faith.

Though the Lord may not remove our burdens, He does give assurance that He will sustain and support us through the problems they present.

> *Have you taken it to Jesus?*
> *'Tis the only place to go*
> *If you want the burden lifted*
> *And a solace for your woe.*   —Hennessay

THOT: God's grace helps you transform weights of fear into wings of faith.

WHEN BURDENS BECOME BRIDGES

For every man shall bear his own burden.

Galatians 6:5

VARIOUS kinds of burdens are mentioned in the Scriptures. Some can be shared, but others God intends that we carry by ourselves. Although the weight of these trials may at times seem unbearable, we eventually come to see that our Lord always has a wise design in the burdens He lays upon us. His purpose is especially evident when we face new crises.

This reminds me of the fable "The Encumbered Ant." The little insect felt he had been given a raw deal because he had to carry a piece of straw that was too long and heavy for him. Creeping wearily across a desert of concrete, he staggered beneath his load. As the stress of the situation increased, the ant became fed up with life. To add to his frustration, he was brought to a halt by a large crack in the pathway. He saw no way of getting across that deep divide. He stood there discouraged. Then a thought suddenly struck him. His backbreaking load could actually be turned into a blessing. Carefully laying the straw across the crack in the concrete, he walked over it and safely reached the other side. His heavy burden had become a helpful bridge!

This story points up a valuable lesson. The burden a Christian is given may be thought of as the weight of God's loving arm upon his shoulder. Through adversity and trial the Lord often provides the resources needed to cross some chasm of difficulty up ahead. If we recognize this and trust in Him, what we originally thought was an unbearable load of care will be used to bring us spiritual progress and victory.

> *Are you burdened, Christian?*
> *Do not sit and fret;*
> *He who gave it to you*
> *Has not failed you yet!*   —Bosch

THOT: Burdens can become bridges to blessings.

3. Chastening and Suffering

Christians are often faced with suffering and distress, but the reason for their trials is not always the same. Both Paul and Jonah were caught in storms, but the circumstances were quite different. To help us understand the meaning of such trials, let's divide them into three main categories.

The first is TRIBULATION—suffering we endure for our Christian witness. This is what the apostle Paul spoke of in Romans 8:35 and 36 when he said, "What shall separate us from the love of Christ? Shall tribulation . . . ? As it is written, For Thy sake we are killed all the day long." See also John 16:33, Acts 14:22, and 2 Thessalonians 1:4-6.

The second is CHASTENING for sin and evil works. This is referred to in 1 Corinthians 11:32, "But when we are judged, we are chastened of the Lord, that we should not be condemned with the world." Hebrews 12:4-11 is a classic passage about our need for this type of loving correction. On rare occasions, sickness may be caused by gross sins of believers who only pretend to be walking in fellowship with the Lord. This is called "the sin unto death"; it is committed exclusively by Christians (1 Cor. 11:28-32; 1 John 5:16). The Lord's chastening of the individual does not mean he will lose his salvation if he fails to repent, but he may first become ill and then eventually lose his physical life. By confessing his sin and changing his wayward tendencies, however, he can bring about his recovery from illness before it culminates in death (Jas. 5:14,15).

Finally, the redeemed may experience HOLY SUFFERING so that God may manifest His glory in their lives. Job was an example of this (Job 1:1,8-12), and so was Lazarus (John 11:4). Other Scriptures which speak of this type of affliction include 2 Corinthians 12:7; Acts 9:16; John 9:2,3; 1 Peter 3:14.

Some miscellaneous reasons for believers having to endure pain and discomfort are: (1) reaping what their parents have sown (Ex. 20:5; 34:7), or (2) incurring physical problems because of what they themselves have sown. These evil acts may have been done before conversion. But according to the natural laws of God, even believers must bear the consequence of such deeds while they are still in their unredeemed bodies (Gal. 6:7,8; Job 4:8; Prov. 22:8).

Christian friend, if you are suffering for righteousness' sake, then be patient and glorify God. Rejoice in the opportunity of showing to men and to Satan what God's grace can do in your life because you have committed your soul to your faithful Creator (1 Pet. 4:19).

Some of the most spiritual Christians have been shut-ins. Charlotte Elliott, the author of the *Invalid's Hymnbook,* never had a well day. Her sweet gospel songs were the outpouring of a heart that knew what it was to suffer according to the will of God. Your "thorn in the flesh" may well be a badge of God's special favor. And if at times you are tempted to become discouraged, recall His sure promise, "No good thing will He withhold from them that walk uprightly" (Ps. 84:11). Indeed, "Our Father's way may twist and turn,/ Our hearts may throb and ache,/ But in our souls we surely know/ He maketh no mistake!"

An unknown poet has written with equal discernment and wisdom:

> Who deepest drinks of sorrow
>   Drinks deepest too of grace;
> God sends the storm, so He Himself
>   Can be our hiding place.

WHEN A BRICK SPAWNED A BOOK

*But as for you, ye thought evil against me; but God
meant it unto good.* Genesis 50:20

THE poet William Cowper has written: "God moves in a mysterious way/ His wonders to perform;/ He plants His footsteps in the sea,/ And rides upon the storm." This suggests that events which seem tragic to us often turn out to be rich blessings from God. The selling of Joseph by his brothers, which eventually brought him to prominence in Egypt, was a wicked act and cannot be excused. Yet in God's overruling providence it became the means of saving the lives of those brothers along with their families. Literally thousands of stories could be told by Christians who have seen triumphs come out of their tragedies.

A modern illustration of this truth is found in the life of Samuel L. Brengle. At one time in his ministry a wicked man attempted to kill him by throwing a paving brick at his head. Brengle survived the dastardly attack, but he had a long convalescent period. During those months he wrote many inspiring articles on the sanctified life. Later, because of their value, they were put into a book entitled, *Helps to Holiness.* It turned out to be his best work and has been widely used. Brengle's wife would say, "Had there been *no brick,* there would have been *no book!*" She was convinced that the Lord had allowed the "tragedy" so that her husband would have time to write. Because of this, she preserved the brick and painted on it the words of our text: "But as for you, ye thought evil against me; but God meant it unto good."

How blessed to know that our Heavenly Father overrules sin and error for His glory and our good!

> *"No gain!" I said, but I forgot*
> *My Father's faithful word,*
> *That all things work for blessing here*
> *To them that love the Lord.* —Beckley, alt.

THOT: Many lives that seem MARRED by accident are actually being MADE by Providence.

THE "OVEN" AND THE "FRYING PAN"

... bring an oblation of a meal offering baked in the oven ... [or] baked in a pan. Leviticus 2:4,5

THE sacrifices described in Leviticus have great typical significance. In the burnt offering we behold Christ dying, but in the meal offering we see Him living! The latter is a picture of our sinless Lord as He walked on the earth. The *fine flour* speaks of the grindstone of suffering that bore down upon Him, so that He was indeed "a man of sorrows, and acquainted with grief" (Isa. 53:3). The *oil* typifies the Holy Spirit's special presence in His life. Leviticus 2 tells us that the fine flour was first *mingled* with oil, and that additional amounts were later *poured* upon it. The mingling speaks of the incarnation—of Jesus' unique deity (Mt. 1:18-23); the pouring depicts the special measure of the Holy Spirit imparted at His baptism when He officially took up His redemptive work (Mt. 3:16). The *baking* suggests the heat of trial that was always a part of our Savior's life, for His holy nature was grieved by the evil that surrounded Him, and by human misunderstanding of His divine mission. He endured anguish too, when He looked ahead to assuming all the sin of the world upon the cross (Luke 22:39-44; Mt. 26:37-42). The oven heat spoke of the hidden sorrows of Jesus' heart, while the frying pan oblation pointed to the trials that were visible to men.

Even today, the more faithfully we follow Christ, the more we will be "persecuted for righteousness' sake." Some of our tribulations will be of the *frying pan* variety—open to the eyes of others. Yet our deepest sorrows will be of the hidden, *oven* variety. But let us rejoice if we are accounted worthy to suffer for His sake!

> *I suffered much for thee, more than thy tongue can tell,*
> *Of bitterest agony, to rescue thee from Hell;*
> *I've borne, I've borne it all for thee,*
> *What hast thou borne for Me?* —Havergal

THOT: Great faith is produced by great trials.

BEATING OUT THE BUBBLES

Behold, as the clay is in the potter's hand,
so are ye in Mine hand.   Jeremiah 18:6

A VISITOR to the shop of a famous potter was puzzled by one operation which seemed to have little purpose. The workman was beating a lump of clay with a large mallet. It looked as if nothing was happening, so the one who was taking the tour finally asked, "Sir, why are you doing that?" "Just wait and watch the results; then you'll understand," was the reply. He heeded the advice and soon noted that the top of the mass began to quiver and swell as little bumps formed on its surface. "Now you can see the need for the pounding," said the man. "I could never shape the clay into a worthwhile vessel if these bubbles remained in it, so I must gradually work them out." The one watching was a Christian, and he immediately recalled Jeremiah, chapter 18. He saw more clearly than ever before why the great Potter must work upon our souls. The discipline of chastening and the trials God sends are necessary to eliminate pride and self-will. This is the way the Master forms us into beautiful vessels prepared to hold the treasures of His grace.

The hymn writer Adelaide A. Pollard may have been motivated by the same thought to pen the words of her enduring hymn, "Have Thine own way, Lord! Have Thine own way!/ Thou art the Potter, I am the clay:/ Mold me and make me after Thy will,/ While I am waiting, yielded and still."

As the hammering blows of trial and sorrow fall upon us in the "Potter's house," let us rejoice, for the undesirable "bubbles" of carnality are being removed to fit us for the Master's use.

> *Beyond our lives the Potter stands*
> *And works His wondrous will;*
> *He shapes the clay with tender hands*
> *And never-failing skill.*   —Anon.

THOT: When God would bring more POWER into our lives, He often brings more PRESSURE.

52

THE NECESSARY "RESTS"

The Lord is good unto those who wait for Him.

Lamentations 3:25

THE tendency to be impatient is in the heart of every human being. Yet we as Christians will experience little progress in sanctification until we accept the Lord's perfect timing in our suffering and learn to rest in Him. The paradox of being told to *"run with patience"* rather than *with speed* (Heb. 12:1) is resolved only when we submit ourselves to God's wise leading. Although at times He may command us to stand still as we face certain "Red Sea" difficulties, our pilgrim march will not be delayed. At just the right moment He will open a special way, providing a shortcut to new plateaus of great blessing (Ex. 14:13-31). Truly, "the Lord is good unto those who *wait* for Him."

John Ruskin once observed: "There is no music in a rest, but the making of music is in it. Our whole life-melody is broken off here and there by 'rests,' and we foolishly think we have come to the end of the 'tune.' God sends a time of forced leisure—sickness, disappointed plans, frustrated efforts—making a sudden pause in the choral hymn of our lives, and we lament that our voice must be silent and our part missing in the music which reaches the ear of the Creator. How does the musician read a rest? See him beat time with unwavering count and catch up the next note true and steady as if no breaking place had come between."

Our responsibility is to learn the "time" and not to be dismayed at the brief but vital interludes of quiet. When God writes the music of our lives, He wisely includes the necessary "rests."

How good it is when weaned from all beside,
With God alone the heart is satisfied,
To hear His voice amid the stillness blest,
And lay me down upon His arms to rest! —Tersteegen

THOT: The STOPS of a good man are ordered by the Lord as well as his STEPS.

DON'T RETALIATE!

*Blessed are ye when men shall revile ... and persecute
you .... Rejoice, and be exceedingly glad.* Matthew 5:11,12

MANY years ago a pioneer missionary to China visited village after village with God's Word. But there was little or no response to his efforts. Finally he said to himself, "My ministry apparently is useless." One day, however, a Chinese student said, "Teacher, I've heard your messages. You speak wonderfully about the Man you call Jesus. I have a spiritual hunger, but before I can make any decision about this One you call Christ, I must have the answer to an important question." "And what is that?" he inquired. "It is this," replied the unbeliever as he struck the missionary a hard blow on the cheek. Stunned and dismayed, the servant of God asked, "Why did you do that?" The young man replied, "I wanted to see how you'd react to an insult—whether you would fight back!" "Retaliation would be wrong," replied the missionary. "My Lord and Savior has said, 'Blessed are ye, when men shall revile you . . . . Rejoice, and be exceedingly glad!'" The student said with a tear, "Teacher, I beg your forgiveness. I've heard those good words of Jesus; but now I've seen them obeyed! Life has taught me to beware of words without meaning. You've brought reality to your teachings. I do want to become a Christian."

Friend, if people unduly criticize you when you're doing the work of Christ, do you rebel or do you rejoice? Jesus said we should be "exceedingly glad" when we are reviled or abused for His sake, for we will have great reward in Heaven. So, when you are hurt or mistreated in the Lord's service, don't retaliate!

Help me, Father, to lift mine eyes
When men unjustly criticize;
Lord, teach me well the precious art
Of "death to self" when tears would start!   —Anon.

THOT: It is more difficult to LIVE as a martyr than
        to DIE as one.

THE MINISTRY OF SUFFERING

This sickness is ... for the glory of God, that the Son
of God might be glorified by it.   John 11:4

NOT all illness is due to chastening. Lazarus became sick through no fault of his own. God just allowed him to suffer and die that Jesus might have the opportunity to call him forth from the tomb. In this way our Lord's divinity was demonstrated to all. Lazarus' death was "for the glory of God."

F. B. Meyer has written, "The child of God is often called to suffer because there is nothing that will convince onlookers of the reality and power of true religion as suffering will do, when it is borne with Christian fortitude .... Everyone cannot be trusted with trial. All could not stand the fiery ordeal. Some who are Christians would speak rashly and complainingly. So the Master has to select with careful scrutiny the branches which can stand the knife, and the jewels which can stand the wheel. It is given to some to preach, to some to work, but to others to suffer!"

Have you ever heard the legend of the mignonette and the gravel walk? The mignonette is a plant that has greenish white spikes of perfumed flowers. "How fragrant you are this morning!" said the gravel walk. "Yes," answered the mignonette, "I have recently been trodden upon and bruised, and it has brought forth all my sweetness." "But," said the gravel walk, "I am trodden on *every day,* and I only grow *harder.*" This commentary on life is quite obvious. Sanctified believers send forth a sweetness that blesses all who come in contact with them, while carnal Christians become hard and bitter under suffering.

How do you react to adverse circumstances?

For every pain that we must bear,
    For every sorrow, every care, there is a reason;
But if we trust Him as we should,
    All will work out for our own good;
    God knows the reason.   —Anon.

THOT: Like the sun's rays ripen fruit, so fiery trials
        promote spiritual maturity.

THE CROSS AND THE GARDEN

Now in the place where He was crucified
there was a garden.   John 19:41

THE first Adam, vibrant with life, lost Heaven for mankind in a verdant spot called Eden. The Last Adam, in blessed contrast, was buried in a similar setting to regain for us that lost inheritance. The cross and its adjacent garden form a golden link in the holy chain forged by grace to redeem man and bind him again to his God in a new and more intimate fellowship.

A most beautiful commentary on this passage came from the pen of Harold C. Phillips: "One might rather have expected to read, 'Now in the place where He was crucified there was a desert.' But not so—it says, 'a garden.' This ugliest of all human deeds, the crucifixion of the Savior, was accomplished where the flowers turned their kindly faces. Near the cross—a symbol of death—was a garden, the promise of perennial, unconquerable life. Nothing is more wonderful than the love Christ had for man, and yet it was this very love, the source of all that was most beautiful in His thought and deed, that sent Him to Calvary. Let us remember too that *God is able to make glorious even those things which are tragic!* Around the cross there is always a garden. To the crucifiers this instrument of death was a symbol of shame and defeat. For the believer, however, the cross was changed by Christ into an emblem of deathless glory."

We who are Christians may be certain that beyond the "Golgotha of darkness" which tests our faith will dawn God's brighter day, for all our sufferings and crosses will have a garden too!

By the cross and the garden—inseparably linked—
  A most wonderful story is told:
For 'tis Christ's death gives life which eternal shall bloom
  In God's city of jasper and gold!   —Bosch

THOT: As the cross had its garden, so each trial has
       its sweet compensation.

OPPOSITION—A MARK OF BLESSING

Woe unto you, when all men shall speak well of you! Luke 6:26
... there are many adversaries.   1 Corinthians 16:9

AS we faithfully serve the Lord through the power of His Spirit, the devil's hosts will begin to attack us, and we may be called upon to suffer for Christ's sake. Russell Ebersole, a veteran missionary, was greatly encouraged by William Pettingill, the beloved Bible teacher. After Ebersole told him of the disappointments and trials he had faced on the foreign field, Dr. Pettingill exclaimed, "Brother, that means you're on the right track. If you never experience any opposition or setbacks in the Lord's work, you ought to get down on your knees and ask Him to show you what you're doing wrong!"

When the bishop of Madras was touring India, he was introduced to a young slave girl who was an outstanding witness for the Lord. Her quiet persistence in telling others of Jesus and His love had won many to Christ. As the bishop looked at her, he saw that her face, neck, and arms were badly scarred. She had received many beatings for her faithful testimony. With tears in his eyes he asked, "Child, how could you bear this brutality?" Somewhat surprised, she replied, "Aren't you glad if you can suffer for Christ, sir?" Her humble response spoke to his heart. It reminded him that if one is true to the Savior, he can expect ridicule and even harsh treatment from the world.

Believer, if all men speak well of you, you may be compromising in some way. But if you are suffering for Jesus' sake, "rejoice, and be exceedingly glad." To encounter opposition in doing God's will is a mark of blessing and promises eternal reward.

If everyone speaks well of you,
It surely would be wise
To check each facet of your life
And weed out compromise.   —Bosch

THOT: If you have the smile of God, you can expect the frown of men.

BRAND-MARKS OF FAITHFULNESS

I bear in my body the marks of the Lord Jesus.

Galatians 6:17

THE day seems to be fast approaching when Christians who stand valiantly for the truth may suffer bodily harm and perhaps even death. Pause and think before you glibly say you'd gladly be a martyr, for without God's enabling grace you'll certainly fail. The sad fact is that many who have made the most self-confident claims of high intention have been the first to defect under fire. See the case of Peter in Luke 22:33,34. Bragging about how strong you'll be in that day is of the flesh (1 Cor. 10:12). Only by humbly relying upon God will you successfully endure persecution.

Paul had to face such hard trials (2 Cor. 11), for the words of our text have literal application: "I bear in my body the scars which mark my bondage to the Lord Jesus!" The apostle may have been thinking of the brands on the flesh of the slaves in those days, when hot irons were pressed against their bodies to mark them as belonging to a certain master.

The great missionary Adoniram Judson battled untold odds to reach the people of Burma with the gospel. Seven heartbreaking years passed before he saw a single convert. Then came war, hunger, and many pain-filled years in Ava Prison. When he was released, he carried throughout his life the ugly scars made by the chains which had bound him. Immediately, he asked the ruler for permission to go into a new area to preach Christ. The request was denied. "My people," said the monarch, "will not listen to anything other missionaries might *say;* but they would certainly take notice of your *scars* and might be converted."

Have you ever really suffered for Christ's sake?

> *O for a faith that will not shrink,*
> *Though pressed by many a foe,*
> *That will not tremble on the brink*
> *Of any earthly woe!*   —*Bathurst*

THOT: SCARS for Christ here means STARS with Christ hereafter!

"THANKSGIVING CORNER"

. . . walk ye in Him, . . . established in the faith,
. . . abounding with thanksgiving.   Colossians 2:6,7

IN her girlhood, Hanna R. Higgins of Australia suffered from a very strange and baffling disease of the bone. As the ailment progressed, she lost the use of her legs, and finally they had to be amputated. For more than 50 years she was bedridden and suffered intensely, yet she bore it with Christian patience. In fact, her life was a benediction to all who came in contact with her. Being well "established in the faith," she abounded "with thanksgiving" and proved to everyone that a believer can be happy even in the most depressing and painful circumstances. In her book *Cloud and Sunshine,* written when she was 77, she said, "I long for all to prove as I do, that with our loving Savior's help it is possible to be happy under very trying conditions." Always rejoicing in the Lord, she learned to call her place of suffering "Thanksgiving Corner." As people visited her, they found her room filled with the glory of God, and they went away blessed. She sent messages to the ends of the earth full of cheer and encouragement. More than 200 foreign and home missionaries were on her prayer list, and she undergirded them with almost unceasing intercession at the Throne of Grace. Handicapped though she was, she sent each of those Christian workers at least one letter of comfort and help every year.

Christian, are you grumbling today about some insignificant little annoyance? Shame on you—shame on *me* if, with all the blessings the Lord has showered upon us, we are not "abounding with thanksgiving"!

> *When you have truly thanked your God*
> *For every blessing sent,*
> *You'll find that little time remains*
> *To murmur or lament.*   —*Anon.*

THOT: Thankfulness revives troubled hearts!

THE "WHY" OF SUFFERING

... ye are in heaviness through manifold trials.

1 Peter 1:6

THE person who must endure suffering will benefit from it if he heeds what the Lord is saying to him. As I look back over my life, I can personally testify that I could easily have done without many joyful experiences. But I couldn't have spared even one valuable spiritual lesson I learned from sorrow! Why? Because, as C. S. Lewis says, "God whispers in our pleasures, but shouts in our pain!" The Lord forces us by our distresses to pay attention to His voice. While times of testing aren't pleasant to endure, we must wait patiently for Him to accomplish His all-wise purposes. If we avoid becoming bitter in our earthly trials, we will learn the lessons of grace which only adversity can bring to the teachable heart.

A. B. Cooper said that one autumn day he went to a chrysanthemum show and saw some wonderful blooms. He asked the gardener, "How in the world do you manage to produce such marvelous flowers?" "Well, sir, we concentrate all the strength of the plant in one or two buds. If we would allow it to bear all the flowers it could, none would be worth showing. If you want a prize specimen, you must be content with a single chrysanthemum instead of a score." For the same reason, God sends trials to prune from our lives the useless blooms of self, popularity, and comfort, so that He may perfect in us one exquisite white blossom of holiness.

Those who accept trouble graciously will grow rich by their losses, rise by their falls, and find new life in Christ by dying to self. This is the blessed answer to the "why" of suffering!

Afraid of troubles? No, but we should think,
"What is God teaching?"—not despairing sink;
Never despond, nor lightly treat the rod,
But fully trust the purposes of God.   —Anon.

THOT: Suffering is sent to sanctify us, not to suppress us.

THE TEST OF FAITH

*Beloved, think it not strange concerning the fiery
trial which is to test you.*   1 Peter 4:12

IN a magazine called *The Teacher*, Pastor Harold Dye
writes about an 8-year-old Mexican boy named Pedro.
One Sunday the lad came up to the minister after
hearing him preach on Simon of Cyrene. "You asked
what we'd do if we had been in the crowd when Jesus
fell under the weight of His cross," said the youngster
earnestly. "I'm sure I would have been happy to help
carry it!" The boy had recently accepted Christ, although his parents were antagonistic to the gospel. To
test him, the minister said, "Yes, but if you had helped
the Lord, the cruel Roman soldiers would probably
have beaten you with whips." Without hesitation the
boy answered, "I don't care! I love Him! I'd have done
it just the same."

Two weeks later, Pastor Dye stood at the door of the
church, greeting the people as they left the service.
When Pedro came by, he patted him affectionately on
the shoulder. Shrinking back with a little cry, the 8-
year-old pleaded, "Please don't do that. My back is
very sore." Since he had barely touched him, the
minister was puzzled. He took the youngster to a
nearby cloakroom and asked him to remove his shirt.
Crisscrossing his back from his neck to his waist were
huge red welts. "Who did that?" the preacher asked
angrily. "My mother. She whipped me because I came
to church!" Pedro had proved he was willing to stand
up for the One in whom he had put his trust. He
wasn't afraid of what anyone could do to him.

The day may come when you will have to suffer for
the sake of Christ. Will your faith stand the test?

> *The fight is on, but be not weary,*
>   *Be strong and in His might hold fast;*
> *If God be for us, His banner o'er us,*
>   *We'll sing the victor's song at last!*   —*Morris*

THOT: Great faith is exhibited not so much in our
ability to *do* as our willingness to *suffer*.

SUFFERING—KEY TO PERFECTION

But the God of all grace ... after ye have suffered awhile,
make you perfect.   1 Peter 5:10

A LADY took voice lessons for years from one of the country's outstanding teachers. Although she could sing with tonal perfection, she was never able to move her audiences emotionally. Her presentations were always cold and mechanical. One day her teacher said, "My dear, I have taught you all I know. But you lack one thing I can't supply. Something will have to break your heart and make you suffer before you will sing with feeling and understanding!" So too, in our Christian experience, suffering and sanctification go hand in hand.

Sir Malcolm Sargent was an outstanding musician. To look at him—a man with a light step and ready smile—one would think life had treated him well, but such an assumption would be in error. Just when he was becoming successful, he collapsed with tuberculosis and had to battle regaining his health while facing financial ruin. Then, when he was returning to the world of music, his beloved 13-year-old daughter was stricken with polio. One night as he was about to begin a performance of "The Messiah," he was handed a note which read, "Your daughter Pam is dying!" With tears in his eyes he walked to the platform and directed the musicians through such tender passages as "Comfort ye, comfort ye My people." Yet out of his sorrows came a deeper sympathy. Sir Malcolm Sargent found the strength to endure suffering in the music of God's Word.

Life has many hard and bitter experiences, but they should make us better Christians; for suffering, when rightly received, is "the key to perfection."

> *He turns sorrow into music,*
> *And our cry to sweetest song,*
> *Weeping to eternal gladness,*
> *Night to day, vast ages long!*   —Rolle

THOT: High spiritual plateaus are reached by way of the lowlands of trial.

62

4. Comfort and Sympathy

Most Christians experience some kind of affliction in life, and when it comes, many questions are asked. The most common one is, "Why did this happen to me?" If we search our hearts and God's Word, we may find the answer, but often it is years later before we discover the Lord's wise purposes. We may even have to wait until we get to Heaven to understand it completely (John 13:7). An unknown author puts it this way: "I know not now why schemes were spoiled,/ And lofty aspirations foiled;/ I know not now why briar and thorn/ Should mar ambitions nobly born./ Hereafter I shall know, shall see,/ These very things were best for me!" Yes, "our light affliction . . . worketh for us a far more exceeding and eternal weight of glory" (2 Cor. 4:17). In the time of suffering, the Holy Spirit pours His healing balm into our hearts to ease the pain through the strengthening "comfort of the Scriptures" (Rom. 15:4).

Our trials and disappointments not only make us seek God's comfort (Ps. 119:34,50), but also cause us to cry out for heartfelt expressions of sympathy from understanding fellow Christians. This is illustrated in the following true incident: A little girl was attempting to enter her father's study and caught her tiny finger in the swinging door. Being a very busy man, her dad was preoccupied with his task and paid little attention to her crying. But he stopped long enough to call downstairs to his wife, "You'd better come up here and look after your child." The mother rushed to the rescue. Taking her small sobbing daughter in her arms, she planted tender kisses upon her brow while she cared for the aching finger. "Does it still hurt badly, dear?" she inquired. "Yes, Mommy, but it hurts worse because *Daddy didn't even say oh!*" Yes, we all need compassion from others when the troubles of life press down upon us.

Sometimes our difficulties take on special meaning for us as God lifts the curtain and shows His providential hand. An old Hebrew legend makes this plain. It tells of a man journeying on a mule through a wild and desolate area. His only companion was a rooster whose shrill crowing at sunrise awoke him to his devotions. At nightfall he came to a small town looking for shelter, but the inhabitants turned him away. Outside the village he found a cave to sleep in. He lit his lamp before retiring, but a gust of wind blew out the light. During the night a wolf killed his rooster and a lion devoured his mule. Early in the morning he went back to the town to see if he could buy some food. To his surprise he found no one alive. A band of robbers had plundered the settlement while he slept and slain all the inhabitants. "Now I understand my troubles," said the man. "If the townspeople had received me, I would have joined them in death. If my rooster and mule had not been killed, their noise and the light from my lamp would have revealed my hiding place. God has been good to me."

Whether we learn why we are suffering affliction now, or whether we have to wait until we get to Glory, we know that the One who went to Calvary to save us would never needlessly hurt or distress us. All is sent in love for our eternal good. A wealthy English gentleman who was deeply impressed with this truth had a

64

beautiful weather vane erected on top of his barn. On it were inscribed the words: GOD IS LOVE. When asked the reason for those words, he replied, "I want to let everyone know that no matter which way the wind blows—God is love!" He said it is not for Christians to judge when the wind is at its best. They must sincerely believe that all is well when God is in it. Sometime later this same Englishman was forced to endure severe affliction, and his friends called to offer their sympathy. Although he was distressed by his circumstances, he pointed to his weather vane and said, "I had that text put up there in my prosperity when all my heart's desires were being realized. And even though the icy winds of trial are blowing now, I'm confident that God's love for me is still the same!" His faith gave him the grace to face the future with confidence.

May these words console your heart: "Love divine has seen and counted/ Every tear it caused to fall,/ And the storm which love appointed/ Is the choicest gift of all!" Let this be your unfailing strength in hours of weakness and tribulation: God has permitted my trouble in His love—a love that never makes a mistake, even though I may not understand the reason for my distress.

Speaking of the often unexplained mystery of suffering, an anonymous poet has written:

> Though providence our comforts shroud
> And dark distresses lower;
> Hope prints its rainbow on the cloud,
> And grace shines through the shower!

CLOUDS, RAINBOWS, AND ANGELS

And it shall come to pass, when I bring a cloud over the earth,
that the bow shall be seen in the cloud. Genesis 9:14

AFTER the flood in Noah's day, the rainbow in the cloud became God's pledge to every living creature that He would never again destroy the earth with water. It was out of the clouds that the deluge came; yet it was upon their retreating shadows that He displayed a colorful arch of promise. Such is the way of our Father in Heaven. It reminds us that very little beauty comes into a human life without the clouds of trial. Unless the sunshine of God's love floods our sorrow with light, there can be no shining rainbow, no beacon of hope in the darkness of human distress. It is in the shadowy mists of trouble that the Lord brings us new blessings and refreshment.

In one of the German art galleries, a painting called "Cloud Lane" hangs at the end of a long dark hall. At first glance it appears to be a huge, ugly mass of confused color, unattractive and foreboding. But when you look closer, you see portrayed on the canvas *an innumerable company of angels.* Theodore Cuyler wrote, "How often the soul that is frightened by trial sees nothing but a conglomeration of broken expectations. But if he analyzes the situation from a position of faith, instead of fleeing away in unbelief and despair, he will soon discover that the cloud is God's wonderful chariot of providence full of angels of mercy."

Never give up if life seems gloomy. The Lord glorifies every billow with His presence, and He sends His angels to help us (Heb. 1:14). Thus He paints our clouds with beautiful rainbows of blessing.

If the dark shadows gather as you go along,
Do not grieve for their coming, sing a cheery song;
There is joy for the taking, it will soon be light—
Every cloud wears a rainbow if your heart keeps right.

—DeArmond

THOT: If your life had no clouds you would never see the rainbows.

JESUS KNOWS AND CARES

And the Lord said, ... I know their sorrows.   Exodus 3:7
In all their affliction He was afflicted.   Isaiah 63:9

GOD knows all about our grief and is deeply touched by it. Indeed, our Lord's loving heart was always filled with compassion when He saw human need. The prophet said of Him that He empathized with them in all their sufferings. The great preacher C. H. Spurgeon declared, "Yes, God is with us in our sorrows. There is no pang that rends the heart and scarcely one that disturbs the body but what Jesus Christ is with us. Do you feel the pinch of poverty? He had no place to lay His head. Do you endure the grief of bereavement? Jesus wept at the tomb of Lazarus. Have you been betrayed? Don't forget, He too had a familiar friend who sold Him for the price of a slave. Never a valley of adversity so dark, so deep, apparently so pathless, but in stepping down you may discover there the footprints of the Crucified One!" As head of the church, Christ feels keenly the things that adversely affect the members of His body.

An anonymous author has written: "He knows the bitter, weary way;/ He knows our striving day by day;/ The souls that weep, the hearts that pray,/ He knows./ He knows how hard the fight has been;/ The clouds that come our lives between,/ The wounds the world hath never seen,/ He knows./ He knows! O thought so full of bliss!/ For though our joys on earth we miss,/ We still can bear it, feeling this,/ He knows!"

Christian, the great Comforter stands ready to wipe away your tears. He will give you grace to carry your heavy burdens. He loves you, and He sympathizes with you in your hour of deepest need.

> *O yes, He cares—I know He cares!*
>   *His heart is touched with my grief;*
> *When the days are weary, the long nights dreary,*
>   *I know my Savior cares.*   —*Graeff*

THOT: Grief is sent to hallow hearts and draw them heavenward.

PRAISE GOD, ELIM FOLLOWS MARAH!

And they came to Elim, where were twelve wells of
water, and threescore and ten palm trees. Exodus 15:27

SHORTLY after the nation of Israel crossed the Red Sea, they came into a wilderness that was parched and dry. Up ahead they saw an oasis of Marah, but their hopes were dashed when they tasted the water and found it bitter and unpalatable. Now note how the Lord met their need. He told Moses to cast a tree into the pool, and lo, "the waters were made sweet" (Ex. 15:25). They were heartened by God's marvelous intervention, and were further encouraged when their next stop was an ideal encampment at Elim. There they found not one oasis but 12 good wells of water in a grove of delightful shade trees.

Israel's experience is analogous to that of the Christian. The tree used by Moses beautifully pictures the cross of Christ, which takes the bitterness out of our deepest trials. In the light of Calvary's love, we can face our difficulties with the confidence that they are sent to promote our growth in grace. Jesus always stands ready to help us bear our burdens, and He works all things together for our good (Rom. 8:28). But that's not all. Along life's way God gives us blessings to compensate for our trials. He knows the journey will be long and hard, so He brings us to places where wells of refreshment strengthen our faith. In the reviving shade of Elim's 70 palm trees, our testimony is renewed and victory is attained.

So cheer up, discouraged pilgrim. God will sweeten the bitter waters of your "Marah" as you look anew to the cross. He will refresh you spiritually by leading you on to a joyous "Elim"!

Elim! Elim! though the way be long,
Unmurmuring I'll journey and lift my heart in song;
Elim! Elim! all my song shall tell
Of rest beneath the palm trees and joy beside the well.
                                                    —*Anon.*

THOT: God-sent clouds are followed by Heaven-sent rainbows.

"LIKE A MAN'S HAND"

Behold, there ariseth a little cloud out of the sea,
like a man's hand.　　　　　　　1 Kings 18:44

MANY unique applications can be drawn from familiar Scripture passages. For example, an unknown author wrote, "It is well if we can see the form of a Man's hand in every cloud that arises in our lives. It is good if we can discern the figure of our Lord, the mighty Maker of Heaven and earth, in every shadow that spreads its wings above us. For then our clouds will leave abundant blessings in their wake, and our dark days will reveal the glory of God in all His protecting and comforting power."

A Christian woman was always so bright and cheerful that everyone wondered at her joyous spirit. "But sister," said a friend, "you must have some clouds in your life." "Clouds?" she replied. "Why of course. If there were no clouds, where would the showers of blessing come from?" This saint of God, like the poet of old, had learned to "trace the rainbow through the rain."

Many believers reach the place of unquestioning faith in Jesus and can sing Joseph Gilmore's hymn with assurance:

> Sometimes, 'mid scenes of deepest gloom,
> Sometimes where Eden's bowers bloom,
> By waters still, o'er troubled sea,
> Still 'tis His hand that leadeth me.

In every cloud that darkens our horizon we may discern the nail-pierced hand of the Man of Calvary. Surely the One who died for us can be trusted to lead and protect us, even in the worst storms of life.

Victory and perfect peace will be yours if by faith you look for the mighty hand of God in your cloud.

> *In all your clouds see the hand of the Savior,*
> *Blessings unnumbered shall flow like a stream;*
> *All for your good He is sending in mercy,*
> *On every billow a rainbow doth gleam.*　　—*Bosch*

THOT: Behind the clouds of trouble the sun of God's grace is always shining.

THE POWER OF PRAISE

And when they began to sing and to praise, . . . they
[the enemy] were smitten.   2 Chronicles 20:22

THROUGH the remarkable incident in the history of the Jewish nation related in 2 Chronicles 20, God gives us a wonderful prescription for victory in the midst of life's adversities.

A great host of pagan warriors had assembled to attack the kingdom of Judah. Not knowing what to do, King Jehoshaphat prayed to the Lord and sought His help. A startling answer to his plea came from a Levite by the name of Jahaziel. Directed by the Holy Spirit, he declared that God would save His people in an unusual way, despite the overwhelming superiority of the enemy. They were to sing praises to the Lord and not give in to worry. The next day, instead of ordering his sharpshooters to advance upon the foe, Jehoshaphat appointed a choir to go before the army! As "they began to sing and to praise," Judah gained a great victory. The people didn't lift a finger; yet through God's intervention all their enemies soon lay dead, and they carried away a great spoil.

Christian, are you up against an insurmountable obstacle? Do you fear that the battle may be lost? Turn the matter over to the Lord, and praise Him for what He is going to do. In this way you'll be letting Him work out the problem, and He will not disappoint you. From your trying experiences you will be able to gather many "precious jewels" that will someday adorn your heavenly crown.

As you give thanks in everything, a song will spring up in your heart, and victory will be assured. So stop complaining, and learn *the conquering power of praise!*

> *Not by cries or groans or fears*
> *Shall life's conflicts here be won,*
> *But by faith that smiles and sings*
> *Ere the battle is begun.*   —Simpson, alt.

THOT: To triumph over trial, stop sighing and start singing!

"THE QUEEN SAID NOTHING!"

... none spoke a word unto him; for they saw
that his grief was very great.   Job 2:13

WHEN Job was in deep trouble, his three friends came "to mourn with him and to comfort him" (Job 1:11). Although they wept, they recognized that his problems were so overwhelming that it would be wise for them to show their concern by just sitting quietly at his side. Therefore we read , "*... none spoke a word unto him;* for they saw that his grief was very great." Their response reminded me of Queen Victoria's expression of sympathy when she heard that the wife of a common laborer had unexpectedly lost her baby. Having experienced deep sorrow herself, she called on the bereaved woman and stayed with her for a while. After she left, the neighbors asked what the royal visitor had said. *"The queen said nothing,"* replied the grieving mother. "She simply put her hands on mine, and we silently wept together."

In my own experience, within the space of just a few weeks the Lord called Home my precious mother, my only uncle, and my closest lifelong friend. How I appreciated the hundreds who prayed for me and encouraged my heart by their acts of love and Christian kindness! God's abundant grace was indeed sufficient for those trying days. Some who were deeply moved expressed their concern by just gripping my hand. They didn't have to make long speeches, for their sympathetic presence and kindly looks spoke volumes.

Like Queen Victoria, if you really care for people who are in trouble, offer a warm handclasp and show them loving concern. This will adequately convey to them your strengthening fellowship and your Christian compassion.

Give me a heart sympathetic and tender,
  Jesus, like Thine; Jesus, like Thine;
Touched by the needs that are suring around me,
  Filled with compassion divine.   Anon.

THOT: Our likeness to Christ can be measured by our
      sensitivity to the distress of others.

OF SYMPHONIES AND EBONY SKIES

God, my maker, . . . giveth songs in the night.

Job 35:10

IN our moments of deepest trouble, how blessed to know that we do not have to create our own midnight melodies! It is *our Maker* who giveth "songs in the night." Never harmonies more sweet than those the Holy Spirit plays. He takes up the harp of God's Word and plucks one string of promises after another as He composes our symphony of comfort! Many saints can testify to the joys they experienced and the unexpected grace the Lord provided when the ebony skies of trial blotted out the glow of their earthly happiness. Paul Gerhardt has written, "For many a raptured minstrel among the sons of light/ Will say of his sweet music, 'I learned it in the night.' "

The great Beethoven lived most of his productive years in partial or total deafness. He was especially concerned because he felt his hearing was essential to creating musical portraits of lasting value. Therefore, when his deafness rapidly became worse, he was frantic with anxiety. Many doctors were consulted and every possible hearing aid was tried, but all was in vain. When the world turned completely silent, he communicated only by means of writing. Yet he found the needed strength to go on. To everyone's amazement, it was only after he lost all sense of outward sound that Beethoven wrote his grandest music! Shut out from the distractions of the world, his soul was flooded with new melodies as fast as his pen could write. *His deafness became his greatest blessing!*

Those who tune their hearts to Heaven, in spite of ebony skies of trouble, will be blessed with new and comforting symphonies of grace.

Songs in the night—ah, such songs the Lord gives!
He's the great Comforter who ever lives;
Though dark without, He sheds wonderful light,
Giving us beautiful "songs in the night."—Brondsema, alt.

THOT: Turn care into prayer, and God will turn midnight into music!

KEEP LOOKING UP!

O Lord, . . . I . . . will look up.

Psalm 5:3

AFTER painting the ceiling of the Sistine Chapel in Rome, Michelangelo found that because he had to look up for so long a time he developed a very stiff and sore neck. He could no longer read or survey blueprints except by holding them above his head. To look down was extremely painful for him. While the consequence of looking up was most uncomfortable physically, it certainly would be a splendid attitude for all of us to assume spiritually. As Christians, we are admonished to "set our affection on things above" and to "look to Jesus." Many of us, however, have cast our eyes downward at material things instead of putting the Lord first. Yet, like Michelangelo, if we are to do our work for God successfully, we must learn to readjust our spiritual sights. The poet has written, "When I look to Jesus, my eyes cannot see/ The troubles and dangers that throng around me./ A look at the Savior, and strength I receive/ To face them with joy, and His promise believe."

If we keep our eye of faith clear by prayer, and our heart steady by resting on God's promises, we'll find the bright lining of His love in every dark cloud. Confident that He knows best and sends only what is needful for us, we will be able to say by His sustaining grace, "I know not the way I am going,/ But well do I know my true Guide;/ So with childlike trust I will give Him/ My hand as He walks by my side./ And as He takes hold of it firmly,/ I quietly say, 'Hold it fast;/ O never allow me to wander,/ But lead me to Heaven at last.'"

> *Don't be downhearted, look up, look up,*
> *For Jesus is on the throne;*
> *And He will supply every need from on high,*
> *Cheer up, cheer up, cheer up!* —Anon.

THOT: When the outlook is dark—try the uplook!

THE COMFORTING STAFF

I will fear no evil; for Thou art with me; Thy
rod and Thy staff they comfort me.   Psalm 23:4

IN the book *A Psalm of an Old Shepherd,* H. W. McLaughlin tells a beautiful story of an experience he had in the land of Palestine. While talking to an elderly sheep herder, he asked how his staff comforted his flock. The man explained that in the daylight he always carried it across his shoulders. This reminded the sheep of his presence, for he had guided and directed them with it when they traveled over a rough stretch of ground or had to pass through a narrow ravine. When night overtook them, or if they were caught in a heavy fog so that the animals could no longer see the staff, he would lower it; and as he walked, he would tap on the ground with it. By the sound of the staff, the sheep were once again guided and comforted. It told them that their protecting shepherd was up ahead picking out a safe pathway. McLaughlin commented, "David must have remembered these things and said in effect to himself, 'It would be unreasonable to suppose that God has less care for me than I have for my sheep.' Therefore, under inspiration, he spoke of the comforting staff."

When the day is bright, we too can clearly see God's "staff of leading." But at other times, when the mist of trouble and the darkness of trial settle around us, we follow *by listening* to His voice through the Scriptures. His inspired Word is therefore a staff of strength as we tread the steep and narrow track that leads upward to the fold of Heaven. Reassured that our Shepherd, though unseen, is still with us, we go forward in faith fearing no evil!

He leads us on by paths we do not know;
Upward He leads us though our steps be slow,
Though oft we faint and falter on the way,
The storms and darkness lead to perfect day.

—*Zinzendorf, alt.*

THOT: All our tomorrows must pass our Good Shepherd before they reach us!

74

GOD'S SUNSHINE ON YOUR FACE

They looked unto Him, and were radiant.   Psalm 34:5
[Show] mercy, with cheerfulness.   Romans 12:8

WHAT a person is *inside* is often displayed on the *outside*. God is light (1 John 1:5), and when His Spirit shines in the believer's heart, some of that inner illumination is bound to manifest itself to others. The faces of Christians who are constantly looking to the Lord Jesus should beautifully reflect the peace and joy that He imparts. The apostle Paul says that this is especially important when we seek to help people in trouble. The expression on our faces can have a profound effect upon the way they react to our help. Arthur S. Way has paraphrased the admonition in Romans 12:8 this way: "If you come with sympathy to sorrow, bring God's sunlight in your face."

You may recall that Job's friends failed completely to do this. Instead of radiating God's joy and light, they enveloped that afflicted saint in a cloud of impenetrable gloom. He therefore called them "miserable comforters" (Job 16:2). Happy is the believer of whom it can be said, "He carries God's sunlight with him wherever he goes!" Glum, long-faced Christians are a contradiction in terms. Instead of encouraging a needy brother and being a shining testimony of what the grace of God can do, they are "sad sack" counselors and poor witnesses.

Let the Holy Spirit flood your life with the Savior's grace and love. Your witness will then become heartwarming and effective as you dispense comfort to others *"with cheerfulness."*

Yes, in this dark world our faces should always reflect God's sunshine.

Carry the sunlight wherever you go,
Let Heaven's joy on your countenance glow;
Men will thank God for the warmth you impart
As love overflows from your radiant heart.   —Bosch

THOT: A gracious smile adds a lot to a Christian's face value!

A SONG OF PRAISE

And He hath put a new song in my mouth,
even praise unto our God.   Psalm 40:3

A PASTOR once went with some foreign colleagues to visit a group of lepers. Wearing sterile robes and protective boots, they walked through cultivated acres which showed the marks of toil. On the way to the chapel where the services were to be held, they passed by the poorly constructed homes of the sufferers. One by one the leprosy victims came, some limping, others in wheelchairs. Their swollen and distorted faces were lifted in happy expectation. They were obviously believers, and were familiar with the hymns of the church. "What shall we sing?" inquired their leader. The pastor and visitors thought they would call for a song like "I must tell Jesus all of my trials." But the guests were surprised when the request was for something quite the opposite. Their favorite selection was this: "The trusting heart to Jesus clings,/ Nor any ill forebodes;/ But at the cross of Calvary sings,/ 'Praise God for lifted loads!'/ The passing days bring many cares,/ 'Fear not,' I hear Him say;/ And when my fears are turned to prayers,/ The burdens slip away./ Singing I go along life's road,/ *Praising the Lord, praising the Lord;*/Singing I go along life's road,/ *For Jesus has lifted my load!*" The pastor and his friends could scarcely keep back the tears when they saw the smiles and looks of spiritual triumph. Their faces were radiant, for they had found that the Lord could give grace and joy in spite of their severe trials.

Christian, do you feel like *sighing* because of life's troubles and sorrows? Try *singing!* Heavenly comfort and God's smile of blessing will brighten your day if you get on the victory side and "keep praising!"

> *Now in a song of grateful praise,*
> *To You, O Lord, my voice I'll raise;*
> *With all Your saints, I'll join to tell,*
> *My Jesus has done all things well.*   —Medley

THOT: The secret of continual revival is the offering of thanksgiving in every circumstance.

"TRY THANKSGIVING!"

Whoso offereth praise glorifieth Me.

Psalm 50:23

MAN was created for the glory of God (Isa. 43:7). Those who are thankful in their attitudes, diligent in their work, and praising in their prayer-life are pleasing in His sight (Ps. 50:23). Again and again the Lord *commands* us to adore Him in all our activities. The book of Psalms closes with an admonition so broad that not a living being is left out of participating in this all-important duty. He says, "Let everything that hath breath praise the Lord. Praise ye the Lord."

A missionary in China was living a defeated life. Everything seemed to be touched with sadness, and although he prayed for months for victory over depression and discouragement, his health remained the same. He finally determined to leave his work and go to an interior station where he could pray and seek victory over his morbid condition. When he reached the new place, he was entertained in the home of a fellow missionary. The first thing he saw was a wall motto which read, TRY THANKSGIVING! The words gripped his heart and he thought, "Have I been praying all this time and not PRAISING?" He stopped and began to give thanks, and immediately his heart was uplifted. Instead of hiding away to pray, and agonizing for days, he immediately returned to his waiting flock to tell them that "praise changes things!" Wonderful blessings attended his simple testimony, and the bands that had bound him and others in a common depression were broken when they began to thank the Lord rather than blame Him—to praise Him rather than pout. TRY THANKSGIVING! "Praise changes things!"

Sound His praises! Jesus who bore our sorrows,
Love unbounded, wonderful, deep and strong:
Praise Him! Praise Him! tell of His excellent greatness!
Praise Him! Praise Him! ever in joyful song! —Crosby

THOT: Thankfulness is the soil in which joy thrives!

COMFORTED BY GOD

In the multitude of my thoughts within me
Thy comforts delight my soul.   Psalm 94:19

HOW reassuring to know that the Lord is abundantly able to carry us through our night of sorrow! Indeed, He is the "God of all comfort" (2 Cor. 1:3). Though His ways may distress us at the moment, they are always right and gracious. So, rather than fretting and complaining, we ought to trust and praise Him. What the Lord has planned for us is designed for our good, and Heaven will reveal that He sent nothing to hurt us—only to bless us. As Christians, we should therefore cast all our care upon the Lord, implicitly believing that He is truly concerned about us (1 Pet. 5:7).

The story is told of a mother trying to calm her fretful daughter. The little tyke had climbed up on her lap, and soon her mother's loving embrace quieted the 4-year-old's uneasiness. But the mother herself was grieving and feeling very sad, for she had just laid to rest her own dear mother, who in days past had been such a spiritual help to her. Looking up, the little girl saw her moist eyes and asked sweetly, "Mama, do you want to be holded too?" Then the mother's tears began to flow freely, and the child hugged her and whispered, "Mama, *God will hold you, won't He?*" The woman was both chided and consoled. Looking to the Lord in her grief, she found grace and solace.

O troubled Christian, turn your problems over to the loving Savior. It's the only way to find peace of mind. Then with the psalmist you too will soon be able to testify, "In the multitude of my thoughts within me Thy comforts delight my soul."

I will commit my way, O Lord, to Thee,
Nor doubt Thy love, though dark the way may be,
Nor murmur, for the sorrow is from God,
And there is comfort also in Thy rod.   —Anon.

THOT: The seeds of God's comfort germinate quickly in the soil of sorrow.

"NO ONE CAME!"

*I watch, and am like a sparrow alone
upon the housetop.*   Psalm 102:7

MAN desperately needs fellowship, not only with God but also with other human beings. One of the most severe forms of punishment, therefore, is solitary confinement. When placed alone in a soundproof room, a person soon experiences hallucinations, undergoes personality changes, and if isolated too long may go berserk. Yes, loneliness is a fearful thing! For that reason, the Lord admonishes Christians to *"visit the fatherless and widows in their affliction"* (Jas. 1:27), and not to forsake the sick and aged in their time of need. Many who are faithful in other ways tend to neglect calling on those who long for fellowship and comfort.

I recently heard of an elderly Christian lady who lived all alone. Partly crippled and confined to her small apartment, she had to rely primarily on the goodwill and help of her neighbors. She spent some of her weary hours keeping a diary, although no one knew why, for she had precious little to record. Finally the Lord called her to Himself to enjoy the blessings of His better Land. It is reported that she lay dead for several days before anyone missed her! Later, in looking through her few belongings, someone discovered her well-worn diary. Most of the book contained little of interest. Near the end of her life, as one monotonous day followed another, pathetically she wrote only these three words on page after page: *No one came!* NO ONE CAME!

The parallel is clear. "Pure religion and undefiled before God and the Father is this: TO VISIT"!

O give Thy sweet concern to me,
  That I may speak with soothing power
A word in season, as from Thee,
  To weary ones in needful hour!   —*Havergal, alt.*

THOT: True sympathy is your pain in my heart.

79

GOD UNDERSTANDS

For [the Lord] knoweth our frame.   Psalm 103:14
His understanding is infinite.   Psalm 147:5

ONE of the things man craves most is to have others appreciate his true attitudes and actions. Many today are crying out, *"No one understands me!"* How comforting to realize that God knows "our frame," is aware of everything we do, and accurately reads our hearts! With joy the psalmist says of the Lord, "His understanding is *infinite.*" Though men may mistreat us and question our motives, we can be sure that the Lord will judge us fairly. We are comforted to know that He weighs our deeds according to His all-wise and loving perception of our efforts and purposes.

In the early days of the automobile, a man's Model-T Ford stalled in the middle of the road. No matter how hard he cranked nor how much he tried to advance the spark or adjust things under the hood, he just couldn't get it started. As traffic began to build up behind him, a limousine pulled in a few cars back, and a wiry, energetic man stepped out and generously offered his assistance. After tinkering for a few moments, the stranger said, "Now try it." Immediately the engine leaped to life! The well-dressed individual then identified himself as Henry Ford. With a smile he said, "I designed and built these cars, so I know what to do when something goes wrong."

In the same way, the God who created us and has providentially planned our lives understands us from A to Z. We can turn to Him with confidence in our dreary hours of frustration, knowing that He recognizes the difficulty of our situation and has the answers to all our problems. We may be at our wits' end, but *God understands!*

> *God understands our heartache,*
> *He knows the bitter pain;*
> *O trust Him in the darkness,*
> *You cannot trust in vain.*   —*Smith*

THOT: God, who MADE you, MARKS your trials and can MEND your troubles.

THY STATUTES—MY NIGHT SONG!

Thy statutes have been my songs.... I have remembered
Thy name, O Lord, in the night.   Psalm 119:54,55

GOD'S people have always found His Word to be a healing balm and a consolation in their hours of distress. Paul referred to the "comfort of the Scriptures" (Rom. 15:4), and the psalmist said that the statutes of the Lord made his heart sing. He called to remembrance the Lord's promises "in the night" when a "horror" of darkness had laid hold upon his soul (Ps. 119:53).

James Creelman wrote about his adventures and passed along this interesting bit of commentary: "On one memorable journey," he said, "I learned for the first time that the world's supply of attar of roses comes from the Balkan Mountains. The thing that interested me most is that *the roses must be gathered in the darkest hours!* The pickers start out at 1 o'clock and finish at 2. At first it seemed to me a relic of superstition, but I investigated the picturesque mystery and learned that scientific tests have proven that 40 percent of the fragrance of roses disappears in the light of day!" God's children also find that the sweetest fellowship and the most fragrant spiritual experiences are distilled in the crucible of sorrow and in the shadows of nighttime adversity! To make melody in the lonely shades of anguish, bewilderment, and sickness requires a song of grace which alone can be put into our soul by the "Chief Musician." As we meditate on God's Word, we echo with joy the words of the psalmist, *"I call to remembrance my song in the night!"*

When the shadows of trial gather, read the book of Psalms until you come to a verse that comforts you. His statutes will become your song and consolation!

> *I stooped to my weary sorrow;*
> *One look at His face divine*
> *Had given me power to trust Him*
> *And say, "Not my will, but Thine."*   —Anon.

THOT: Christ commands us to believe His daylight at midnight!

HELP FOR OVERWHELMED SOULS

When my spirit was overwhelmed within me,
then Thou knewest my path.   Psalm 142:3

WHEN we are crushed under adverse circumstances, we can find sweet comfort by simply resting in the Lord. He will sustain us in His boundless love and guide us back to the paths of peace.

One day a robin flew into our home through the partially opened sliding door that divides our dining area from the shaded back porch. Frightened by its confining new environment and my wife's excitement, the distressed bird fluttered frantically about the room. It hurled itself against the windows and screens in an effort to regain its freedom until it was exhausted. With glassy eyes and beak open wide, it perched on the back of a chair as if it had given up. At that point I gently took hold of the trembling creature. Petting its head and back, I took it outside and released it. Quickly it flew back to its nest in a nearby tree. Confident and safe, the robin soon began to sing again.

This incident reminded me of the story of a woman who had become distraught by her seemingly impossible predicament. While reading Psalm 142, she realized that even though she felt frustrated and defeated, the Lord would quiet her spirit if she would just stop struggling and rest in Him. Yielding herself to God, she found peace and the way out of her troubles—just as that robin had allowed me to comfort and deliver it from its distress.

Believer, are you overwhelmed by adverse circumstances? God knows all about it. Ask Him to strengthen and direct you. Then, like that bird, you will soon be singing songs of relief and gladness.

The clouds hang heavy round my way, I cannot see;
But through the darkness I believe God leadeth me;
'Tis sweet to keep my hand in His while all is dim,
And then with faith and courage bright, just follow Him.
—Anon.

THOT: It takes the storm to prove the real shelter!

THE SINGING HEART

*And at midnight Paul and Silas prayed, and sang
praises unto God.* Acts 16:25

THE plight of Paul and Silas was dismal. Their backs were bleeding from the cruel beating they had received, their feet were imprisoned in the stocks, and they were restricted by chains in a dark dungeon. Yet we hear no complaints, but prayers; no sighs, but songs! Such is the triumph of faith over circumstances—of spiritual joy over physical handicaps. The body can be imprisoned, but not the redeemed soul! By the power of Christ it can soar above its troubles and breathe the pure oxygen of Holy Spirit power! Victory through grace bursts the bands of trouble and leads others to the One who imparts to His children supernatural joy (Acts 16:26-34).

Mr. Robinson, a detective, had to go down into a coal mine to get some evidence. When he got to the bottom of the shaft, he asked the supervisor where he could find his client. "Oh, you'll have no difficulty," said the man. "He's sure to be singing." As Robinson went along the dank corridor of the mine, he said to himself, "Surely, if a man would be singing here, it must be a dreary hymn like: 'Plunged in a gulf of dark despair/ We wretched sinners lie.'" He had not gone very far when he heard a cheery voice raising this triumphant strain: "I've reached the land of corn and wine,/ And all its riches freely mine;/ Here shines undimmed one blissful day,/ *For all my night has passed away.*" That's what the grace of God can do!

Will you grumble at every little inconvenience and problem that arises today, or will you raise a hymn of praise? God grant us singing hearts!

> *My Savior comes and walks with me,*
> *And sweet communion here have we;*
> *He gently leads me by His hand,*
> *For this is Heaven's borderland.* —Stites

THOT: The truest expression of Christianity is not a sigh but a song!

THE BIBLE'S EASY CHAIR

*... all things work together for good to them
that love God.* Romans 8:28

IN her autobiography Fanny Crosby comments about the doctor who unwittingly caused her blindness: "I've heard that this physician never stopped expressing his regrets, and that it was one of the sorrows of his life. But if I could meet him now, I would say, 'Thank you, thank you, over and over again for making me blind.' Although it may have been a blunder on his part, it was no mistake on God's. I believe it was His intention that I should live my days in physical darkness, so as to be better prepared to sing His praises and incite others to do so." By a doctor's mistake, God therefore gave to the church the wonderful heritage of the blind Fanny Crosby. With her increased spiritual insight, she wrote hundreds of inspiring and enduring hymns.

A visitor went to see an elderly lady who had very few earthly possessions—just a bed, an old chair, a table, a stool, and a cupboard. After a little while the guest asked, "Do you ever feel like murmuring at your difficult lot?" "Well, sometimes Satan does tempt me to complain, but then I just ask the Lord to put me into my easy chair, and to keep me quiet." The visitor looked around to see what she could mean, but all he saw was the hard stool and the broken armchair. "I don't see any easy place for you to sit," he said. "No, you misunderstand me," said the precious old saint. *"My easy chair is Romans 8:28.* It's always close by. When I need it, the Lord just sets me into it and I'm at rest. Then I say to Satan, 'Now you be quiet!'"

Christian, don't sit on the edge of the stool of worry; relax in the restful rocker of Romans 8:28.

> *I sing because I'm in His care,*
> *The Father's love is everywhere,*
> *I'm in His care—may this thought bring*
> *A trustful peace through everything. —Simpson*

THOT: God often gives us crosses here that we may wear crowns over There.

84

CHRISTIAN SYMPATHY

. . . weep with them that weep.

Romans 12:15

IF we truly love the Lord, we can't help but sympathize with those who have sustained a deep sorrow. It is a consolation to them to see compassionate tears in the eyes of a friend and feel his warm handclasp. Love doesn't need many words to express its feelings. When members of the body of Christ suffer, all true believers should suffer with them.

D. L. Moody once said that he became accustomed to attending funerals of children because of his large Sunday school class. "I became hardened to it like a doctor," he said, "and I could go to them without any sympathy. One day one of my little scholars was drowned, and the mother sent word that she wanted to see me, so I went. I had my 4-year-old daughter with me. And when we got outside she asked, 'Suppose we were poor, and I had to go down to the river for sticks, and should fall in and get drowned, and you had no money to bury me, would you be sorry, Papa?' Then, looking up into my eyes with an expression that I'd never seen before, she asked, 'Did you feel bad for that mother?' I clasped her to my heart," said Moody, "and kissed her. My true sympathy was awakened."

Do you sympathize in Christlike kindness and affection with those who are passing through the "valley of weeping"? If in the desert of sorrow you can create an oasis of heavenly comfort and consolation by your spiritual admonitions, the benediction of Psalm 84 will rest upon you, "Blessed is the man . . . who, passing through the valley . . . make it a well" (vv. 5,6).

Give me, O God, a heart of understanding
And quick discernment others' griefs to see;
Then let me be a source of consolation
To those who, wordless, seek for sympathy. —Anon.

THOT: Measure your likeness to Christ by the range of your sensitiveness to the sorrow and pain of others.

HOW GOD MAKES COMFORTERS

Blessed be God . . . who comforteth us . . . that we may be able to comfort them who are in any trouble.   2 Cor. 1:3,4

LITTLE wisdom is acquired in days of prosperity and carefree happiness, but what marvelous lessons we learn in the university of pain and tears! We discover that God has a special key of consolation to fit every lock of sorrow. Only after experiencing His comfort are we fully prepared to help our fellowmen. J. W. Bramhall says, "Sorrow can lead us into one of four lands: the *barren land* in which we try to escape from it; the *broken land* in which we sink under it; the *bitter land* in which we resent it; or the *better land* in which we bear it and become a blessing to others."

An elderly Chinese philosopher was approached by a young woman who was griefstricken because she had lost her only son. "I will be able to help you," he said, "if you bring me some mustard seed; but you must get it from a home where there has never been any sorrow." Eagerly the woman started her search. In every place she visited, however, there had been trials or the loss of a loved one. Returning, she exclaimed, "How selfish I've been! Sorrow is common to all." "Ah," said the sage, "you have learned a valuable lesson. You have acquired a wealth of wisdom that not only has eased your own grief, but has also prepared you to sympathize with others."

If the God of all comfort has consoled you, Christian, and given you fresh perspectives of His grace, don't hoard up that precious treasure. Having experienced His balm of healing, use it to help those by your side who need compassion and understanding.

Have you known the blessing of the comfort of the Lord,
Learned a needed lesson thru the healing of His Word?
Share the consolation that has warmed your weary soul,
And its joyous ripples will to others surely roll.   —Bosch

THOT: God doesn't comfort us just to make us comfortable but to make us comforters!

"WE LEPERS"

And whether we be afflicted, it is
for your consolation.   2 Corinthians 1:6

GOD has a special purpose in sending sorrow and trials into our lives. He doesn't grieve us needlessly but desires to purify and shape us according to His holy will. As we learn the lessons afforded by suffering, we are better able to teach others how to bear their burdens and appropriate the "comfort of the Scriptures" (Rom. 15:4). In Jesus Christ we find the grace we need to profit from sickness, loss, and distress. By yielding to Him in our difficulties we learn compassion for others who are going through similar experiences. We can then be used effectively to encourage their hearts by giving them the consolation they so desperately need.

A missionary in the Hawaiian Islands who had worked for 11 years among the lepers of Molokai wrote a letter to the Christians back home. He urged them to pray for the poor souls with whom he labored. As he penned the words, "The lepers here are so needy," he suddenly stopped as if paralyzed. He noticed for the first time a small white spot on his hand which indicated that *he himself had contracted the disease.* With deep emotion he crossed out the word *"The"* and wrote, "WE lepers." Not until that moment did he truly enter into the mental agony of those who were suffering so much. Sustained in his own tribulation by the Holy Spirit, he took up his work among the afflicted people of Molokai with greater sympathy and effectiveness than ever before.

If God has comforted you, He wants you to pass the blessing on to others who are treading the rugged path of affliction.

> *O give forth the oil of His comfort*
> *That fell on your wounds like a balm,*
> *That hearts which are bowed and so broken*
> *May grow patient and strong and calm.*   —Anon.

THOT: Trials can transform ordinary Christians into extraordinary saints.

87

KNOCKING OUT THE PROPS

We are . . . cast down, but not destroyed. 2 Corinthians 4:8,9
. . . underneath are the everlasting arms. Deuteronomy 33:27

THE apostle Paul went through many trials in his Christian life. We read that he was distressed, perplexed, persecuted, and cast down. But he didn't despair, for he knew that God would sustain him. Other passages of Scripture show that no matter how much the apostle was deprived of possessions, friends, and freedom of action, he never lost courage. He knew he could always count on the Savior for support. When he was put in prison for preaching the gospel of Christ, he was not bitter—even though he was forsaken by his friend Demas who loved this present world. Instead he joyfully exclaimed, "Notwithstanding, the Lord stood with me" (2 Tim. 4:17). O that we might attain the same heights of sanctification! Amid the decaying assets of this present world, we can be assured that the Lord will undergird and strengthen us.

"Look, Dad," said a small boy walking with his father by the river, "they're knocking the props from under the bridge. Why are they doing that? Won't it fall?" "No," said his father, "they just want the structure to sink down on those big stone piers. That will give the bridge the permanent support it needs."

Sometimes earthly things are taken away so that we come to rest upon God's everlasting arms—which can bear any weight. Once we recognize this truth, we will exclaim like Paul, "We are . . . cast down, but not destroyed."

Christian, when the Lord allows the props to be knocked out from under you, He's just trying to get you to settle down in the strong arms of His comforting presence.

> *God the Eternal is your refuge,*
> *Let it still your wild alarms;*
> *Underneath your deepest sorrow*
> *Are the everlasting arms.* —*Anon.*

THOT: The steps of faith fall on the seeming void, yet they rest on the Rock beneath.

THE MELODY WEAVERS

*. . . be filled with the Spirit, . . . making melody
in your heart to the Lord.*   Ephesians 5:18,19

SOME of the most beautiful carpets in the world are made in India. I was surprised to learn that most of this intricate weaving is done to the sound of music. The unique designs are handed down from one generation to another, and each pattern has a tune of its own. In fact, the instructions for making these rugs are outlined on pages of script that resemble sheets of music. First the foundation cords are stretched on a great wooden frame, and a group of workers are seated on a long bench behind this webbing. Then the music begins as the master in charge gives directions for each stitch in a strange chanting tone. Even the colors to be used are denoted by the particular rise and fall of his voice as he sings the unusual and haunting aria.

As I pondered that bit of information, I realized that we too are weavers. Day by day we intertwine the threads given to us by God—some dark, some bright—into the pattern that makes up the design of our lives. As we are filled with the Holy Spirit, and He echoes the melody of grace in our hearts, the product we fashion in response to His voice turns out to be a thing of beauty. Every strand is woven progressively into the fabric according to His perfect plan (Rom. 8:28).

Are you allowing the wave-notes of God's love to color your thoughts and deeds today so that your testimony becomes an increasingly beautiful tapestry of grace? If you weave to the melody of a singing heart, the world will stop to note your praise-filled life and glorify your Father in Heaven.

> *I weave to melodies divine*
> *God's colors, both the drab and bright,*
> *Until by grace my life becomes*
> *A tapestry fit for His sight!*   —Bosch

THOT: God's song in your heart should be seen in your face and evidenced in your good works!

I WANT NO MORE?

*I count all things but loss for the excellency of the
knowledge of Christ Jesus, my Lord.* Philippians 3:8

WHEN Pilate had to declare Jesus' guilt or innocence,
he said, "I find no fault in this man" (Luke 23:4). His
negative response merely stated what he did NOT see
in Christ. In contrast, we who have accepted the
Savior can speak positively, for we find in Him all the
fullness of grace and truth. Once we are enlightened
by the Holy Spirit, we recognize that nothing is so significant in life as fellowship with Jesus. Paul gladly
spurned worldly gain that he might enjoy a deeper
relationship with the risen Lord. "The excellency of
the knowledge of Christ" was his primary concern. If
you itemize the things most precious to you, how far
down the list would the name of Jesus appear?

After meeting one of God's servants who had the
same aspirations as the apostle Paul, an unknown
poet penned this touching biography: "In the heart of
London city,/ 'Mid the dwellings of the poor,/ These
bright, golden words were uttered,/ *'I have Christ!
What want I more?'/*Spoken by a lonely woman/ Dying
on an attic floor,/ Having not one earthly comfort—/
'I have Christ! What want I more?'/ He who heard
them ran to fetch her/ Something from the world's
great store;/ It was needless—died she, saying,/ 'I
have Christ! What want I more?'/ But her words will
live forever;/ I repeat them o'er and o'er. God delights
to hear me saying,/ 'I have Christ! What want I
more?'/ Look away from earth's attractions;/ Friend,
those joys will soon be o'er;/ Rest not till your heart's
exclaiming,/ 'I have Christ! What want I more?'" Can
you honestly echo those words?

> Once it was the blessing, now it is the Lord;
> Once it was the feeling, now it is His Word;
> Once His gifts I wanted, now the Giver own;
> Once I sought for healing, now Himself alone.

—Simpson

THOT: Jesus Christ is not valued at all until He is
valued above all!

"WHATE'ER OF EARTHLY BLISS..."

In everything give thanks; for this is the will of
God ... concerning you.   1 Thessalonians 5:18

THIS scriptural command is difficult to obey! Once we learn the lesson, however, we find it to be the high road to perpetual joy and peace in the Holy Spirit — despite life's often depressing events. Each new trial eventually proves to be a blessing, for our Heavenly Father takes away the evil effects and makes the experience profitable to us. According to our text, we are not totally yielded to the will of God if we fail to give thanks for the problems that seem to be contrary to our shortsighted desires.

Back in the 18th century, a young woman by the name of Anne Steele encountered one trial and disappointment after another. A devout Christian, she always attempted to raise a song of praise in her night of distress. Finally she was subjected to the "acid test." Engaged to be married, she had looked forward to the day with eagerness, making all the preparations with joy and happy anticipation. The hour arrived and so did the guests, but the wedding had to be delayed because the groom was missing. Some time later, a messenger brought the tragic news that the man to whom she was betrothed had drowned. Her sanity almost fled at the sudden shock, but after a while she regained her spiritual composure and then she penned this hymn, which is still found in many hymnbooks: "Father, whate'er of earthly bliss Thy sovereign will denies,/ Accepted at Thy Throne of Grace, let this petition rise:/ Give me a calm, a thankful heart, from every murmur free;/ The blessings of Thy grace impart, and make me live to Thee."

Do you give thanks in *"everything"*?

> *O Thou whose bounty fills my cup*
> *With every blessing meet,*
> *I give Thee thanks for every drop —*
> *The bitter and the sweet!*   —Crewdson

THOT: If you are wearing "a spirit of heaviness," try exchanging it for "a garment of praise"!

91

HE FEELS AND UNDERSTANDS

For we have not an high priest who cannot be touched
with the feeling of our infirmities.   Hebrews 4:15

OUR Savior knows all about our suffering because He once lived here on earth as a man. Being "touched with the feeling of our infirmities," the Lord Jesus can fully identify with us in our distresses.

Someone put up a sign: PUPPIES FOR SALE. Among those who came to inquire was a young boy. "Please, Mister," he said, "I'd like to buy one if they don't cost too much." "Well, son, they're $25." The boy looked crushed. "I've only got $2.05. Could I see them anyway?" "Of course. Maybe we can work something out." The lad's eyes danced at the sight of those five little balls of fur. "I heard that one has a bad leg," he said. "Yes, I'm afraid she's crippled for life." "Well, that's the puppy I want. Could I pay for her a little at a time?" The man responded, "But she'll always have a limp." Smiling bravely, the boy pulled up one pant leg, revealing a brace. "I don't walk good either." Then, looking at the puppy sympathetically, he continued, "I guess she'll need a lot of love and help. I sure did. It's not easy being crippled." "Here, take her," said the man. "I know you'll give her a good home. And just forget the money." The boy's own experience had given him a deep feeling for the puppy.

That is a limited but accurate illustration of our Savior's sympathetic understanding. Having suffered Himself, He has a compassion far beyond human measure.

Believer, Jesus is touched by your distress and grief. Trust yourself to His care. His arms of love will enfold you and carry you through every trial.

> *No one understands like Jesus,*
> *Every woe He sees and feels;*
> *Tenderly He whispers comfort,*
> *And the broken heart He heals.*   —*Peterson*

THOT: God's heart is touched when your heart is
    tried.

"HOW FAVORED I AM!"

... be content with such things as ye have; ... I will
never leave thee, nor forsake thee. Hebrews 13:5

A CERTAIN widow managed to support herself on a very slim budget by knitting and sewing for others. The house in which she lived was more than a hundred years old, and time was fast taking its toll. As one room after another became uninhabitable, she closed it — until she lived in only one. She didn't dare to have a fire when the wind blew hard because the chimney had crumbled so much that it was unsafe. *"How favored I am!"* she said. "When it was the coldest, the wind didn't blow much, or else there was so much snow on the roof that I could have a fire without danger. I can't be thankful enough." When asked if she was lonely living way out of town where her house was, she said, "Oh, no, I get along very well. Throughout the day my Bible is always lying open nearby to comfort me, and at night I can see the neighbors' lights. That's enough company for me. I've heard much about sick people this winter," she continued, "but I think how favored I am, that I can sleep all night in health."

Some years later, rheumatism disabled her feet, but she continued sewing, always with one swollen, painful limb raised upon a cushion. *"How favored I am!"* she still exclaimed. "When my daughter Lydia was alive, I lost the use of *both* feet for a time, but then she was here to take care of me. Now that she's gone, the Lord has partially restored one leg so I can get around again. I can't help thinking, 'What if it had been my hands the Lord had disabled?' Oh, *how favored I am!*" Trusting that Friend who never forsakes His own, she was content with circumstances as they were. *Are you?*

> *Give me a calm, a thankful heart,*
> *From every murmur free;*
> *The blessings of Thy grace impart,*
> *And make me live to Thee.*   —Steele

THOT: We all live in one of two tents: con-tent or discon-tent.

A CHRONIC COMPLAINER CURED

*Casting all your care upon Him; for He
careth for you.*   1 Peter 5:7

INSTEAD of giving their cares to Jesus, many people
have a habit of reciting them to others. By incessantly
repeating them, they become increasingly depressed
and their listeners are soon wearied of their lament-
ing. Mary Bachelor was at one time a chronic complainer. The daughter of a minister, she kept house
for her brother who was also a clergyman. The constant unloading of her troubles upon him became so
disturbing that one day she noticed lines of care beginning to etch themselves upon his face. Turning to the
window in remorse, she saw some tall poplar trees
framing the setting sun and casting dark shadows
across the lawn. "I'm like those trees to my brother,"
she thought, "I'm always casting shadows. *Why don't I
bury my sorrows by leaving them with Jesus?*" She
went to her room and found relief in tears, after which
she wrote this hymn lyric: "Go bury your sorrow, the
world has its share;/ Go bury it deeply, go hide it with
care,/ Go think of it calmly, when curtained by night;/
Go tell it to Jesus, and all will be right./ Go tell it to
Jesus, He knows all your grief;/ Go tell it to Jesus,
He'll send you relief./ Go gather the sunshine He
sheds on the way;/ He'll lighten your burden—go,
weary one, pray." Later, when she became a more
cheerful Christian, her verses were printed in a local
newspaper. Philip P. Bliss set them to music, and the
song has since been sung around the world.

Mary Bachelor, a chronic complainer, had found the
cure for her depression by casting her care upon Jesus
and leaving it there. So may you, dear friend.

Hearts growing aweary with heavier woe
Now droop 'mid the darkness—go comfort them, go!
Go bury your sorrows, let others be blest;
Go give them the sunshine; tell Jesus the rest!—Bachelor

THOT: If you're on the rocks, don't despair—be a
       lighthouse!

5. Death and Heaven

The Bible gives us very few details about the believer's life in Heaven immediately after death. But enough is revealed to cheer our fainting hearts, to awaken our highest aspirations, and to stimulate us to be diligent in serving Jesus. We are told that entering the Lord's presence will be blissful, for Philippians 1:23 says that "to depart and to be with Christ . . . is *far better.*" The Scriptures also teach us that we'll be reunited with friends and loved ones who have gone before. What comfort this brings to our souls!

Shortly before his departure for the celestial realms, evangelist Dwight L. Moody made a triumphant statement that sparkles with faith—a kind of faith that should be the portion of every Christian. To one of the last audiences ever to hear him preach, he said, "Friends, someday soon you will hear the news that Dwight L. Moody of Northfield is dead! Don't you believe a word of it! I shall be more alive then than I ever was." Such should be the sunset glow in the believer's heart at the end of life's journey.

John Bunyan in his dying hour clung to the same truth that sustained Moody, and he penned these lines: "They are not dead, those loved ones who have passed/ Beyond our vision for a little while;/ They have but reached the Light, while we still grope/ In darkness where we cannot see them smile./ So let us gird our souls with this bright hope,/ Still praising God as bravely here we wait;/ Then, loving, serving, till our Father calls,/ We'll find our dear ones waiting at the gate."

At another time Bunyan wrote, "All our loved ones who died in Christ are triumphantly singing hallelujahs in the highest Heaven. While we are fighting and sighing here below, they are rejoicing with Jesus above. According to His prayer for them, they are seeing His glory" (John 17:24).

When Christians die, they do not *"pass away,"* they *pass into Heaven itself,* there to enjoy the rich fellowship that God has promised them. Based on His Word, we can declare with conviction that the best is yet to be!

An anonymous poet summarized the glorious prospect awaiting the Christian with these triumphant words:

> When we reach our peaceful dwelling
>   On the strong eternal hills,
> And our praise to Him is swelling,
>   Who the vast creation fills—
> When our paths of prayer and duty
>   And affliction all are trod,
> And we wake to see the beauty
>   Of our Savior and our God—
> Oh, 'twill be a glorious morrow
>   To a dark and stormy day,
> When we smile upon our sorrow
>   And the clouds have passed away.

THE HOME BEYOND THE RIVER

*I pray thee, let me go over and see the good land
that is beyond the Jordan.* Deuteronomy 3:25

THESE words of Moses express his keen desire to
enter the promised land, and they always remind me
of the closing hours of Dr. M. R. De Haan's fruitful
life. One day I went to visit him at his home, where he
was confined with a severe heart condition. A week
earlier he had lapsed into unconsciousness and experienced the trying moments that usually characterize
a death struggle. Unexpectedly, however, he rallied
and seemed to be some better. Reflecting on this, he
told me he was greatly disappointed, for he longed to
be with Jesus. He had always anticipated Heaven, but
now the desire "to depart and to be with Christ" had
become exceptionally strong. Looking out the window,
I commented on the lovely view he had of the
Thornapple River as it flowed placidly behind his
home. "Yes, it's magnificent," he said, *"but everything
looks different and even more beautiful when you're
standing right on the bank!"* His soulful expression
conveyed his deeper feelings concerning his imminent
Homegoing. As a physician, he recognized that he was
right on the brink of the river of death, and he wanted
me to know he had no fear in his heart—only a holy
and deep longing to experience the eternal pleasures
that await the redeemed. I offered a word of prayer,
and he clasped my hand for a meaningful moment as
our visit ended. Two hours later Dr. De Haan's struggling heart suddenly stopped and he entered the promised land of rest.

As a Christian, do you view death as a glorious
release from sin and sorrow? Remember, many blessings are reserved for you just "beyond the Jordan."

> *I've a home beyond the river,*
> *I've a mansion bright and fair;*
> *I've a home beyond the river—*
> *I will dwell with Jesus there.* —Peterson

THOT: Death is only a shadow on life's river where it
meets the great eternal sea.

HOME BEFORE DARK

Behold, now the day draweth toward evening, . . . get you early
on your way, that thou mayest go home.   Judges 19:9

I WANT to make an application from this passage to
bring home a truth about the Christian's departure
for the "many mansions." James McConkey told this
story: "One day I dropped in on an old friend—one of
God's dear saints. Rich in experience, she was ripe for
the coming glory. She had gone so far in life's pilgrimage, however, that her mind was slightly beclouded
and her memory affected. As I rose to leave, she exclaimed, 'I want to go home, too.' Then with a tender
smile she said with a profound touch of pathos in her
voice, '*I want to go home before it gets dark.*' I opened
the door and started on my journey. The twilight was
still aglow with the vanishing beauty of the sunset.
Beyond lay the glory of the Heavenly Father's house.
My soul was tingling with the spiritual message my
dear friend's words had just brought me. What an unspeakable blessing for God's children *to reach Home
before it gets dark!* Before the darkness of a broken
body and failing health; of dimmed senses and clouded
faculties; of physical suffering and infirmities; of
vanished faces, voices, and fellowship—before all of
these come, how blessed it is to 'reach Home before it
gets dark'! Sometimes we deplore the passing of those
of God's own who die young . . . . how premature it
seems. But we are mistaken, for they have simply
reached the splendor of His glory ahead of us."

Yes, when our loved ones unexpectedly leave for
Heaven, our heartstrings are torn. But remember,
God has just allowed them to get on their way early,
while the sunset glow of health is still with them, so
that they will arrive Home before dark.

> *My heavenly home is bright and fair;*
> *No pain, or death can enter there*
> *Its glitt'ring tow'rs the sun outshines;*
> *That heavenly mansion shall be mine.* —Anon.

THOT: Death for the Christian is not bane but blessing, not tragedy but triumph!

PULLING HEAVENWARD!

... the child ... is dead ... I shall go to him,
but he shall not return to me.   2 Samuel 12:22,23

IT is blessed to know that when our saved loved ones depart they await us on the heavenly shore and will someday welcome us into the "everlasting habitations" (Luke 16:9). David experienced this comfort at the death of his little child. He anticipated a blessed reunion with him in Paradise, for he consoled himself with the soul-assuring words, *"I shall go to him."*

Many people have been drawn heavenward by the same thought. J. Wilbur Chapman told a lovely story illustrating this. After a meeting one night a man grasped his hand and said, "Listen to my story. I once had one of the best positions in this city, but strong drink was my destruction. I was lying helpless in the gutter one day when someone shook me and cried, 'If you want to see your boy alive, hurry home!' His words sobered me. As quickly as I could, I went up to the squalid apartment where my wife and boy had been forced to live because of my sin and degradation. I found that a heavy truck had struck the child and he was dying. He pulled me down by his side saying, *'I will not let you go, father, until you promise to meet me in Heaven!'* He then gasped for breath a few times and was gone. They had to forcibly break away his grip on this hand of mine," said the father, "and from that day until this I have felt him *pulling me heavenward.* Today I am redeemed and looking forward to meeting my boy in Glory!"

In my mind's eye I can see you, dear reader, nodding in agreement and saying, "Yes, there's a hand that is also beckoning me to that better land!"

Beautiful hands of a little child, see!
Waiting in Heaven, O loved one, for thee;
Rosy-cheeked darling, the light of your home,
Taken so early, is beckoning, "Come"!   —*Anon.*

THOT: You must receive God's man here if you want to be received into God's mansion hereafter!

SATISFIED AT LAST

I shall be satisfied, when I awake, with
Thy likeness.   Psalm 17:15

MY grandfather Henry VanderWerp was a preacher, poet, and songwriter. A fearless, warmhearted servant of the Lord, he looked forward to seeing his Savior. Like Abraham, he was looking for a "better country," where bliss is untinged by sorrow. Because the words of Psalm 17:15 were so precious to him, his family had that text inscribed on his tombstone as his final testimony.

According to the commentators, this Scripture text of joyous assurance has two meanings. First, it refers to the tremendous thrill that will be ours *when we see Christ's face.* Second, the phrase "when I awake, with Thy likeness" indicates that *when we receive our new resurrection bodies,* which will be like His "glorious body," we will be fully and eternally satisfied.

Bishop Thoborn tells a touching story about the only photograph he had of his child who had died. The picture was imperfect and so blurred that scarcely a trace of the true features could be seen. In desperation he took it to an artist and asked if he could do anything to restore it. Three weeks later he received a sharply detailed and neatly framed picture. He was startled with its clarity, for it was just as if the child were again before him. The image had actually been in the old photo, but it had been concealed by blurs and mists. So too, in each of us is the image of the Lord, but it is dimmed and clouded by the blemishing effects of sin. Someday, however, Christ will cause His likeness to shine forth from us in radiant splendor! Beautiful in His image, we shall be *satisfied at last!*

> *What will it mean to see at last the Savior,*
> *He who in love for man so freely died?*
> *I shall awake that morning in His likeness,*
> *And—waking thus—I shall be satisfied.*   —Anon.

THOT: For the Christian, death is awakening from a night of sorrow to the day of eternal bliss.

TRUSTING JESUS ON DEATH ROW

Yea, though I walk through the valley of the shadow of death,
I will fear no evil; for Thou art with me. Psalm 23:4

A READER of *Our Daily Bread* who works at Philadelphia College of the Bible sent me this true story: A young man named Charlie was involved in a ruckus in which the matron of Haverford College was killed. He was soon sentenced to death for the crime. While confined in jail, he was gloriously saved through the work of a gospel team from the Aldan Union Church. The team leader from the Bible college had the joy of visiting him in prison because he had taken their correspondence course. Having a beautiful tenor voice, he had also taken an interest in sacred music. His favorite selection was "No One Ever Cared for Me Like Jesus." Just before he went to the electric chair, he was asked if he had any special requests. He said he would like to speak to the other prisoners in the exercise yard. When the privilege was granted, he told the men of his joy in the Lord and testified that he had no fear about his impending execution. He expressed his regret, however, that he had waited until he got into prison to learn the way of salvation. He concluded his testimony by singing his favorite hymn. The *Philadelphia Bulletin* reported that he repeated it courageously all the way from death row to the electric chair. As the black hood was pulled down over his head, the last words that came from his lips were these: "*Till someday I see His blessed face above!*"

Yes, Charlie entered the valley of the shadow of death without fear, for Jesus had taken "the sin and darkness" from his heart and was walking with him. If death should knock at your door today, would you have the same testimony?

No one ever cared for me like Jesus,
There's no other friend so kind as He;
No one else could take the sin and darkness from me,
O how much He cared for me! —Weigle

THOT: You need not fear death's darkness when Christ the Light is with you.

GRACE TO FACE THE GRAVE

I will fear no evil.

Psalm 23:4

ONE day evangelist D. L. Moody was criticized by someone who had heard him speak on the subject of Heaven. "Preacher, you talk so confidently about the blessing of being 'called Home to be with the Lord,' but tell me, are you ready to die right now?" Moody looked at his critic thoughtfully and replied, *"I'm prepared* to die because I have accepted Christ as my Savior and He has given me eternal life. But I must frankly admit that *I'm not ready* to die at the present moment. God has given me *living grace* now to do His work, and I'm sure that when my time comes He'll give me *dying grace.*" As Moody predicted, his last hours were filled with peace and victory. At the end he seemed to look into Heaven itself, for he said he could see his loved ones waiting for him there.

When I was a boy of 9, I was told that the doctors had given up hope for my recovery from tuberculosis. I already knew the Lord Jesus as my Savior, but the thought of dying troubled me. I said nothing to my distressed parents, but I talked to a sympathetic uncle about my fears. He laid his hand on mine and quoted those comforting words of Psalm 23. Then he said very tenderly, "Henry, maybe the Lord will spare your life, and that's why now you have only 'living grace.'" The Lord did restore me, and He has given me 58 additional years, most of them spent in the Lord's work. Uncle Jake was right. I didn't get dying grace because it wasn't needed then.

If you are living for the Savior now, you can be sure He'll give you grace when you face the grave.

God promises grace for that moment
When I must pass death's dreaded door;
His presence will lighten the valley
Until I reach Heaven's bright shore.   —Bosch

THOT: Take care of your life and the Lord will take care of your death.

THE HARMLESS SHADOW

Yea, though I walk through the valley of the shadow
of death, I will fear no evil.   Psalm 23:4

IN this verse David is not speaking of walking TO the valley or even IN the valley, but he says, "Yea, though I walk THROUGH the valley." For the child of God, the tomb is not the end of the line; it's the junction where he leaves earth's sin and sorrow behind and boards the chariot bound for eternal bliss.

Our text also speaks of the "shadow" of death. This has great significance, for shadows are actually harmless. Yes, we may dread them and shrink from them, but they cannot hurt us. The shadow of a dog can't bite, nor can the silhouette of a sword wound us. Ivor Powell wrote in *Bible Pinnacles,* "Shadows are not possible unless a light is shining somewhere; and this shadow of death mentioned in Psalm 23 is cast across the valley by the Light of the World Himself who waits to welcome His homecoming pilgrim."

An elderly Christian was in much distress as he lay dying. "Pastor," he said, "for years I have relied upon the promises of God, but now in the hour of death I can't remember a single one to comfort me." Knowing that Satan was disturbing him, the preacher said, "My brother, do you think God will forget any of His promises?" A smile came over the face of the dying believer as he exclaimed joyfully, "Oh, no! He won't! Praise the Lord, now I can fall asleep in Jesus. I know I can trust Him to remember them all, and bring me safely to Heaven." Peace flooded his soul, and a short time later he was ushered into Glory.

Don't fear death, child of God! Christ took its real sting, and for you it is now just *a harmless shadow!*

Beyond the shadows, the face of Jesus,
With Him forever in endless light;
His glorious presence shall be my portion
Beyond death's shadow, beyond earth's night.

—Gilmore, alt.

THOT: For the Christian, DEATH is the last shadow before Heaven's DAWN!

103

"GOODNIGHT"—NOT GOODBY

Weeping may endure for a night, but joy
cometh in the morning.   Psalm 30:5

FOR several years I worked in the summer months with my father, who was superintendent of the Garfield Park Cemetery in Grand Rapids. During that time I witnessed many graveside services. I'll never forget the one that was held for the small daughter of a minister who had been a pastor in this city. He and his wife had prayed for a child for many years and finally were blessed with a baby girl. She was a beautiful youngster, and everyone loved her. Her parents were overjoyed with this treasured gift from the Lord. Then at the age of 6 a tragic accident took her life. After the funeral in their local church, the body was brought to Grand Rapids for burial. Because the family was so well known, the public was allowed to attend the committal service. A large crowd had gathered, and the coffin was opened once more. Even in death the child was a picture of loveliness, her long curls cascading down to her shoulders. As the parents stood gazing at her lifeless form, a holy radiance seemed to light their faces. Then the father raised his hand heavenward, and with tears rolling down his cheeks he said, "Goodnight, darling, we'll meet you in Heaven. We loved you much, but Jesus loved you more. Goodnight!" Not a dry eye could be seen.

That godly pastor and his wife were living in the hope of the resurrection. They knew that weeping endures for a night, but joy comes in the morning.

Has a loved one recently been snatched from your embrace? I trust that for you it was not an eternal goodby, just a sweet "goodnight."

Only "goodnight," beloved—not "farewell!"
A little while, and all His saints shall dwell
In hallowed union indivisible—
Goodnight! goodnight! goodnight!   —Doudney

THOT: Christ has made death but a starlit strip between friendships of yesterday and reunions of tomorrow.

NOURISHED BY TEARS

My tears have been my food day and night.

Psalm 42:3

WHAT a strange yet beautiful text this is! Imagine being *nourished by tears!* Even though sorrow may be our daily portion, eternity will reveal that we gained more strength and spiritual stature through these trials than we did in times of prosperity. We do not grow when we taste only the shallow experiences of temporal happiness.

The poet wrote: "Once I heard a song of sweetness as it cleft the morning air,/ Sounding in its blest completeness like a tender, pleading prayer./ And I sought to find the singer whence the wondrous song was borne,/ And I found a bird sore wounded, pinioned by a cruel thorn./ I have seen a soul in sadness while its wings with pain were furled,/ Giving hope and cheer and gladness that should bless a weeping world./ And I knew that life of sweetness was of pain and sorrow borne,/ And a stricken soul was singing with its heart against a thorn!/ We are told of cruel scourging, of a Savior bearing scorn,/ And He died for your salvation with His brow against a thorn./ Ye are not above the Master. Will you breathe a sweet refrain?/ Then His grace will be sufficient when your heart is pierced with pain!"

The prophet Isaiah wrote many centuries ago, "And though the Lord give you the bread of adversity, and the water of affliction, yet . . . thine ears shall hear a word behind thee, saying, This is the way, walk ye in it" (Isa. 30:20,21).

May we not shun the Heaven-sent nourishment of sorrows, but humbly let them draw us closer to the Savior. Yes, earthly tears can be sustenance for our souls and jewels for our eternal diadems.

All that He blesses is our good,
And unblest good is ill;
And all is right that seems most wrong
If it be His sweet will.

—*Faber*

THOT: Grief is itself a medicine, and food for the soul.

105

SONGS IN THE NIGHT
... in the night His song shall be with me.

Psalm 42:8

A FORMER missionary tells how African Christians express their sympathy when death touches the home of a believer. Unlike some of us who glibly quote some Scripture verse and repeat certain cliches, they show their deep concern by sitting quietly with the bereaved family. Knowing that words are often empty and meaningless at a time like that, these Christians enter into the grief of their friends by tears and warm, understanding looks of love. But as the night shadows deepen, the mood changes. Instead of wild dancing and beating of drums, which was their custom before they became believers, they open their hymnals and begin to raise their voices in reverent singing. Every selection in the book, from joyous gospel songs of testimony to more subdued hymns of comfort and adoration, are rendered a cappella. The singing continues all night, and both young and old take part. By the time the last song is concluded, the sun has risen and the morning burial service takes place. Through the long hours of darkness, great blessings and spiritual help are brought to the bereaved family. They have been pointed to the One who is the source of all comfort and reminded of the joys being experienced by their loved ones in Glory.

Child of God, if you have recently suffered a deep sorrow in your life, take a cue from those African believers. Pick up a hymnbook and begin to sing or read aloud the lyrics penned by great Christians. The biblical teachings and admonitions they express are priceless (Col. 3:16). You'll be richly comforted by those inspiring songs in your night of grief.

> *Throughout the hours of darkness dim,*
> *Still let us watch and raise a hymn;*
> *And in deep midnight's thoughtful calm,*
> *Pour forth the soul in joyful psalm.*   *—Anon.*

THOT: Praising God in sorrow can turn your midnight into music.

"DEAR JESUS, TAKE CARE OF ME!"

For this God is our God forever and ever; He will be our guide even unto death.　　Psalm 48:14

SEVERAL years ago an Indian girl named Jenny was taken to a missionary hospital in New Mexico to receive treatment for rheumatic fever. This 11-year-old child loved the Lord and cherished her hymnbook and Bible. Although physically weak, she was always kind and cheerful. In fact, the head nurse often said Jenny seemed too sweet and angelic for this evil world. But her health did not improve; instead, she continued to lose weight. Part of the problem was her enlarged, diseased tonsils. So an operation was absolutely necessary. Surgery would be dangerous, but Jenny trusted her Savior and was not afraid. A touching thing happened while she was on the operating table. As she was losing consciousness, she whispered quietly, *"Dear Jesus, take care of me!"*

Later the missionary said, "We shall never forget those words, for they were the last she ever spoke. After the surgery was completed and they were about to wheel her back to her room, Jenny stopped breathing. There was no struggle. The Lord just quietly took her to Heaven. Everyone was heartbroken, but when the Indian children sang 'Safe in the Arms of Jesus' at her funeral, we realized that her prayers had really been answered. *Jesus was taking care of her in a most glorious way,* for He was showing her all the wonders of His mansions above!"

O for the faith of that little Indian girl! As we repeat her simple prayer, "Dear Jesus, take care of me," we can find a rainbow in every dark cloud and the sparkle of God's love in every tear as He gently leads us Home.

> *God, give me the faith of a little child*
> *Who trusts so implicitly,*
> *Who simply and gladly believes Thy Word,*
> *And never would question Thee.*　　—*Showerman*

THOT: Faith builds a bridge across the gulf of death!

HOMEGOING

Thou shalt guide me with Thy counsel, and afterward
receive me to glory. Psalm 73:24

SOMEONE has written: "Because the Lord bought us with His blood, sought us by His Spirit, and distinguished us by His grace, we may be sure that He will keep us by His power, guide us by His counsel, and then honorably introduce us to Glory." It is comforting to know that God is leading, and that *death for the Christian will not be sunset but dawn!*

Martha Snell Nicholson once wrote, "I stood with God on the edge of the world, and my hand was in His hand./ I looked down the road of the past, as it stretched away in the dim distance,/ Till it was shrouded in the mists of time./ I knew it had no beginning,/ And a little chill wind of fear blew about my head./ God asked, 'Are you afraid?'/ And I said, 'Yes, because I cannot understand/ How there can be no beginning.'/ So God said, 'Let us turn and face the other way.'/ And I looked into glory, and my heart rejoiced with joy unspeakable./ And then my mind went ahead, a billion, billion years,/ And I knew there would be no end,/ And again that little chill wind of fear began to blow./ And God asked me again, 'Are you afraid?'/ And I answered, 'A little, because I cannot understand/ How there can be no end.'/ So God asked me tenderly, *'Are you afraid now, today, with your hand in Mine?'*/ And I looked up at Him and smiled and replied,/ 'O my Father, no!' And God said,/ *'Every day in eternity will be today!'*"

Yes, He who guides us today will receive us into Glory tomorrow! Praise His Name!

> *When I am called from life's hard school,*
> *Cleansed by His blood from sin,*
> *Then may He say to me, "Well done"—*
> *Eternity with Him!*　　　　　　　　*—Anon.*

THOT: The soul united to Christ cannot be completely at rest til it arrives at the heavenly home.

ENTERING THE DESIRED HAVEN

*He maketh the storm a calm, . . . so He bringeth them
unto their desired haven.*   Psalm 107:29,30

A BEAUTIFUL young girl lay dying of an incurable
disease. Although she was a Christian, she was filled
with fear. When her pastor arrived, she cried out in
her anxiety, "Oh, Pastor Donald, I am desperately
afraid of what's ahead. I feel as if I am being thrust
out of my happy young life into the darkness. I can't
see anything, and my faith is so weak I can't seem to *believe anything!* What shall I do?" The preacher's
solemn face grew very tender as he looked at her. He
knew she was a true child of God and that Satan was
attacking her in her final moments. He said, "A year
ago a sweet, lovely baby came into your sister's household. Do you remember all that was done for her?
Everyone in the family tried to think of something
they could do for that tiny bit of helpless humanity.
Dainty dresses and a lacy bassinet were made ready
before she came. Special formula was prepared, and
the love that was displayed to assure her comfort was
wonderful to behold. That is the kind of care we give
to a new life when it comes into this world. *Do you suppose God is any less loving than we?* In that Home He is
calling you to enter, He too has arranged everything
necessary for your happiness, and He will make you
feel perfectly at ease!" A light broke over the face of
the dying girl. "I see what you mean," she said. "He
went to 'prepare a place' for ME!" Her last moments
were spent in peace, and there was a smile on her lips
a few days later when she went to be with Jesus.

If Jesus is your pilot, you too will someday anchor
safely in the beautiful harbor of Heaven.

> *Just beyond life's surging breaker*
>   *Looms the Land of peace and rest;*
> *Few more days and we are welcomed*
>   *In the haven of the blest.*   —*Kuipers*

THOT: The closer we come to the celestial harbor, the
brighter the beams of the great Lighthouse
shine upon us.

THE DEATH OF A LITTLE BOY

Even so it is not the will of your Father ... that one
of these little ones should perish.   Matthew 18:14

THE death of a little child stirs our deepest emotions and awakens our tenderest sympathies. Yet the believer can find consolation and hope through God's Word. In mourning the passing of his infant son, King David was comforted by the thought of meeting him again, for he exclaimed, "I shall go to him."

Mae Rose has written a touching poem about the Homegoing of her nephew's small son. We share it with you, praying that it will speak to your heart. "The days are long since Jesus took our precious, blue-eyed boy;/ We thought that he was ours to keep—our hope, our pride, our joy./ His little feet had scarcely felt the roughness of life's road/ When by his side we sadly knelt—our tears, how fast they flowed!/ So oft in play he paused intent, as though some voice to hear;/ Then, hand and face upraised, content—'twas angels lingering near!/ That tiny finger pointing up to God from whom he came—/ Such memories sweeten sorrow's cup whene'er we speak his name./ *'Bobby's up There,'* from coma deep his blue eyes opened wide/And speaking thus, he 'fell asleep,' with angels by his side./ It seemed life's fairest dream was crushed that hour—that night so still;/ More plainly now, our spirit hushed, we see our Father's will./ In love He loaned Heaven's flower fair; in love He came to reap/ That blossom sweet we shared awhile—'twas ever His to keep./ Our darling's safe, for he's with Him! Today faith bids us tell—/ E'en though our eyes with tears may dim, *'our God does all things well!'*"

Sorrowing mother and father, rejoice! Your sweet baby is safely home with God.

> *God wants some little rosebuds*
> *For His garden up above!*
> *So oft He gathers children*
> *To the mansions of His love.*   —*Bosch*

THOT: Over the grave of each baby, Jesus writes the epitaph: "Of such is the kingdom of heaven!"

GRANDPA'S LAST HYMN

And when they had sung an hymn, they went out.

Matthew 26:30

AS our Lord faced the awful prospect of dying on the cross, He concluded the first communion service with the singing of a hymn. By this He showed believers that when they have faith in God and His sustaining grace they can meet the "last enemy" with confidence and joy.

Grandpa Bosch was a dear saint who experienced this peace as he came to the end of his life. I remember hearing my parents tell of his final moments. Shortly after the turn of the century, grandfather became afflicted with a serious heart ailment. In spite of all efforts by the doctor to relieve his condition, he steadily grew worse. After three trying days and nights, he realized that death was near. Calling his children to his side, he had a loving word for each of them. Then he said, "Let's part with a hymn." His weak voice quavered as he sang, "My hope is built on nothing less than Jesus' blood and righteousness." But it seemed a bit stronger when he came to his favorite third stanza, "His oath, His covenant, His blood support me in the whelming flood; *when all around my soul gives way, He then is all my hope and stay.*" With tear-filled eyes the others joined in on the chorus, "On Christ, the solid rock, I stand—all other ground is sinking sand. All other ground is sinking sand." After a tender word of spiritual admonition, grandpa closed his eyes and went to be with the Lord.

If we live for God daily and rely upon Him, then in the face of death we too will have the peace my grandfather had when he sang that parting hymn.

> *When darkness veils His lovely face,*
> *I rest on His unchanging grace;*
> *In every high and stormy gale,*
> *My anchor holds within the veil.* —*Mote*

THOT: Death for the Christian is the golden key that opens the palace of eternity.

111

THE SWEET AWAKENING

And He took the child by the hand, and said unto her,
Talitha cumi.   Mark 5:41

TO emphasize the importance of the raising of Jairus' daughter, the Holy Spirit recorded the story in several places. Luke's account does not use that fearful word "death" in describing the young girl's departure, but substitutes a sweeter expression which promises a glorious awakening. Comfortingly our Lord declared, "She sleepeth!" Some say that in the original dialect the words Jesus spoke to raise this beloved daughter to life were the same terms of endearment often used by mothers in awakening their children. What Jesus said when He tenderly took the cold, still hand of the child in His own may have been, *"Little lamb,* I say unto thee, arise!" Perhaps they were the same words she was accustomed to hearing in the morning from her parents. This reassures us that there will be nothing fearful about our glad awakening in Heaven. It will all be *just as natural as rising from sleep!* The love which blesses us here will also greet us there!

One commentator says: "She saw strange, but friendly faces—those of Peter, James, and John. She beheld the dear, familiar countenances of those she knew best and loved most—her father and mother. And greatest of joys, she looked into her Savior's face—commanding, serene, loving, and gracious. *So shall it be with us in that wonder-hour for which we wait!* We shall find ourselves with the people of God in an everlasting kinship. We shall see again those loved ones from whom death parted us for a brief time; and best of all, we shall find ourselves with Him!"

Yes, those who fall "asleep in Jesus" (1 Th. 4:14) immediately experience a calm, sweet awakening!

> *Asleep in Jesus! peaceful rest*
> *Whose waking is supremely blest;*
> *No fear, no woe shall dim the hour*
> *That manifests the Savior's power.*   —*Mackay*

THOT: Death is gain because it means: Heaven, happiness, home, and Him! HALLELUJAH!

"HOWDY, JOHN! THANK YOU, JOHN!"

*Make to yourselves friends . . . , that . . . they may receive
you into everlasting habitations.*   Luke 16:9

THE Bible teaches that the souls we influence or lead
to Christ will not only be a joy to us in Heaven, but
they will also welcome us into our eternal home. John
A. Broadus, renowned scholar and seminary professor
known for his deep piety, was apparently motivated
by this prospect, for he testified to people in all walks
of life about Jesus' saving power. One of the first men
he spoke to was a red-haired fellow by the name of
Sandy Jones. The young farmer held back and would
only say, "Well, I don't know. Perhaps someday I'll
become a Christian." Then one night in a church service the continuing witness of Broadus bore fruit.
After giving his life to the Savior, Sandy walked
across the old-fashioned meetinghouse, held out his
hand, and said gratefully, "Thank you, John. *Thank
you so much!*" Eventually Broadus left the area, but
whenever he returned home in the summer, this first
convert would walk up to him, stick out his large,
rugged hand, and say, "Howdy, John! I'll never forget
you, John." As a result, their hearts were knit together
in love. Later, after Sandy had died and the beloved
teacher himself was on his deathbed, he said to his
family, "I think when I get to Heaven, the sweetest
sound to my ear, next to the welcome of my Savior,
will be the greeting of Sandy Jones as he thrusts out
his big hand and says again with a grateful smile,
'Howdy, John! Thank you, John!'"

How many will be waiting on Heaven's bright shore
to receive YOU into God's "everlasting habitations"
because you helped lead them to Jesus?

> *And when with my glorified vision at last*
>   *The walls of that City I see,*
> *Will anyone there at the beautiful gate*
>   *Be waiting and watching for me?*   —Hearn

THOT: Heaven's sweetest welcome awaits the soul
    winner.

A MANSION APARTMENT

*In My Father's house are many mansions.... I go
to prepare a place for you.* John 14:2

AS a young man, I often misinterpreted this verse and said, "Jesus is preparing a *mansion* for me." Then one day I read the text more carefully and noticed the word "are" in John 14:2 for the first time. I realized then that the mansions were already made when Jesus spoke these words. What He is doing now is preparing A PLACE—a special apartment in those sparkling palaces—which will be particularly suitable for me. Understanding this truth helps to dispel the believer's fear of leaving this life.

An elderly preacher who secretly dreaded death was powerless to console others facing that prospect. Eventually he moved from the area where he had ministered for a long time. But when all his household goods had been placed in the van, he lingered in the home where his children had been born, and where he had enjoyed so many blessed hours of communion with the Lord. Just then an intimate acquaintance who had been helping with the packing came and tapped him on the shoulder. "Pastor," he said, "come with us; *your new home is much better than this one.*" The man didn't know it at the time, but he had preached a powerful "sermon" to his friend. His words caused the minister to see that his home in Heaven would be far superior to the things of this world. After that, the pastor no longer dreaded dying.

Yes, right now Jesus is preparing a special place for each of His children in those eternal mansions! Although we cannot fully grasp the wonder of it all, we need not fear death, for our "new home" will be so much better than anything this world has to offer.

O Paradise, O Paradise, how I long to see
The special place my dearest Lord has prepared for me;
Lord Jesus, King of Paradise, keep me in Your love
And bring me to that place of peace when we meet above.

THOT: Lord, while You are preparing a place for us,
prepare us for that place!

DEATH—THE KEY TO A PALACE

*In My Father's house are many mansions.... I go
to prepare a place for you.*   John 14:2

A MOTHER of two said that one evening as she was
tucking her small daughter in bed the child exclaimed,
"Mother, stay with me while I go to sleep." Remember-
ing all the tasks that still awaited her, she hesitated.
But when she saw the troubled look on the youngster's
face, and knowing her dread of the creeping darkness,
she sat down by the bedside and caressed her daughter's soft hand in her own. Soon the child drifted away
to dreamland. As the mother sat there, the Lord
brought home to her heart a blessed and comforting
thought. Bowing her head, she prayed, "O Lord, when
life's evening comes, bring before me all Your good
promises, so that by grace I too may be able to say
with a childlike trust, *'Father, take my hand—stay with
me while I go to sleep.'* Guide me safely in the valley,
and then receive me to Glory." In the light of John
14:2, this is a prayer every Christian can express with
confidence.

Someone has said, "God conceals from us the full
happiness that follows death so that we may be able
to endure life!" Today you may be sorrowing for a
loved one whom God has called home to Heaven, but
actually it is for yourself that you weep. Believers
who die are blissfully happy in the place Jesus has especially prepared, and we are really selfish if we wish
them back in this land of the dying. John Milton has
well said, *"Death for the believer is the golden key that
opens for him the palace of eternity!"*

Meditate on John 14:2. If you think of the joy your
Christian loved one is now experiencing in Glory, it
will put a rainbow in the cloud of your sorrow!

Weep not because I walk no longer with you,
    Remember, I am walking streets of gold;
Weep for yourselves that you awhile must tarry,
    Before the blessed Lord you may behold.   —*Ryberg*

THOT: We think of death as a going away, but for
    the Christian it is really a wondrous arriving!

115

TO BE WITH HIM IS HEAVEN!

We are ... willing ... to be absent from the body,
and to be present with the Lord. 2 Corinthians 5:8

A CHILD of God who was seriously ill and lacked assurance of salvation said to his physician, "Doctor, although I'm a Christian, I'm afraid to die. Exactly what happens to us in the hour of death?" The surgeon, who was also a believer, thought for a moment and then replied, "I'm afraid I can't give you an exact answer to that question!" As he walked across the room to leave, he desperately wished he could say something comforting. Pausing briefly before opening the door, he heard the sound of scratching and whining on the other side. Suddenly he realized that he had left his car window open and his little dog had jumped out. With the patient's permission he let in his pet poodle, who leaped on him with an eager show of gladness. In a flash the doctor's mind was awakened to a scriptural truth he had never before put into words. Turning to the sick man, he said, "Did you see how my dog acted? He's never been in this room before. He had no idea what was inside; yet when I opened the door, he sprang in without fear, for he knew his master was here! As Christians, we have not been told much about the glories that await us on the other side of death. But one thing we do know: *our Master is there, and that is enough!* When the gate opens to eternity, you and I need not cringe in terror; for to see His face will make us supremely happy."

The Bible assures us that to be "absent from the body" is to be "present with the Lord." This truth should give every believer blessed comfort in the hour of death, for to be with Jesus will be Heaven's greatest joy!

> *O how blessed is the promise,*
> *When our spirit is set free,*
> *To be absent from the body*
> *Means to live, O Lord, with Thee!* —Bosch

THOT: The heart of Heaven is Jesus; the more we love Him, the more we long to be there.

A CHANGE OF RESIDENCE

We are ... willing ... to be absent from the body,
and to be present with the Lord. 2 Corinthians 5:8

THE little book entitled *Walter Doesn't Live Here Anymore* impressed me deeply when I read it years ago. It was a touching account of an earnest preacher, greatly loved by all, who was taken from a fruitful ministry at the age of 34 by a sudden illness which caused his death. At the time his brother Clarence Walker wrote this memorial booklet, people were singing the popular song, "Annie Doesn't Live Here Anymore." This title suggested to the author a spiritual truth that brought solace to his heart. He found great comfort in knowing that his loved one was not really dead but had just changed his residence from earth to Glory. Clarence told about his brother's becoming critically ill and being taken to the hospital. He wrote, "When I arrived at his bedside, he was dying; yet he was singing, praying, and even witnessing to those nearby. I said to him, 'Walter, you must be quiet and rest.' For a while he would be still but not for long. Then his condition worsened, and suddenly he left this life and moved from his tenement of clay to be with Jesus. As I gazed upon his face, I remembered the words of Paul that to be 'absent from the body' is to be 'present with the Lord.' The blessing this brought to me found expression as I said to myself, ' *Walter doesn't live here anymore!* He has gone to Heaven, and his earthly house is empty.'"

As you bring to mind your loved one today who has died in the Lord, don't think about his mortal remains, but remember that he "doesn't live here anymore." Like Walter, he has changed his residence to dwell in the bliss of the blessed Savior's presence.

> *Then say not, "He is gone!"*
> *Nor think of him as dead;*
> *But say, "In Father's house*
> *He has arrived," instead!* —*Anon.*

THOT: If to live means grace, then to die means Glory!

A PLACE "FAR BETTER"

... having a desire to depart and to be with Christ,
which is far better.   Philippians 1:23

FOR the believer, death is a glorious entering into the presence of Christ. Free from sin at last, the child of God basks in the "pleasures forevermore" which the Lord has prepared for all who love Him. Then why do we make our funerals so sad and even at times morbid? Shouldn't we rejoice that another weary pilgrim has reached Home? Especially when the Bible tells us that compared to the very best this world has to offer, Heaven is FAR BETTER!

Many years ago the *Presbyterian Magazine* carried this story: "London has never witnessed such a funeral service as was held for F. B. Meyer in Christ's Church Cathedral. There was not a single note of defeat, no hint of tragedy, no suggestion of regret. Instead, there were radiant Scripture messages and glorious Easter hymns. At the close of the service the vast congregation stood with bowed heads expecting the organist to play the usual throbbing dirge of the 'Death March.' Instead they heard *the triumphal notes of the 'Hallelujah Chorus'!* And why should it be otherwise, when a great servant of Christ was standing at attention before his King? That is the faith which is ours today! We do not worship a dead Jesus, but a living Christ, 'who hath abolished death, and hath brought life and immortality to light through the gospel'" (2 Tim. 1:10).

Sorrowing Christian, lift your eyes heavenward. You may weep for your own loss, but you should rejoice that your saved loved one is *now standing "faultless before the presence of His glory with exceeding joy"* (Jude 1:24).

Passing out of the shadow, into the purer light;
Stepping behind the curtain, getting a clearer sight.
Passing out of the darkness, into eternal Day;
Why do we call it dying—this sweet going away?—Anon.

THOT: Every lock of sorrow has a key of promise to
          fit it.

DON'T GRIEVE—BUT GLORY!

. . . ye sorrow not, even as others who have no hope.

1 Thessalonians 4:13

OUR loved ones who have gone to be with the Lord are far better off in the joy of Christ's presence than if they had remained on earth (Phil. 1:23). Therefore, we should not wallow in sorrow nor make ourselves weak from self-pity. Yes, we may grieve over our deep personal loss, but we must not focus our attention on the grave. Rather, we ought to lift our eyes heavenward, where that dear one is enjoying unending delights—no longer troubled by this sinful world. The Homecoming of the Lord's saints is precious to Him, and we shouldn't selfishly want to keep them from His company. Let's rejoice that the Savior has brought them safely to Glory, and that He will return to reunite us with them in Heaven's eternal day.

As I was thinking of the time I would depart this life and go to be with Christ, I penned this bit of verse entitled, "I've Climbed the Golden Stair": "When I have heard the heavenly choir/ And left this temporal shore,/ I'll thrill with rapture here unknown/ As Jesus I adore./ Old friends I've known long years ago/ Will bid me welcome Home;/ Delighted in that bliss I'll rest,/ This earth no more to roam./ What joy will be my portion then/ All free from sin and pain!/ With death forever past for me,/ *Don't wish me back again./* When you see this old shell of mine,/ Don't think that I am there;/ I've traveled on to live with God—/ I've climbed the golden stair!"

Bereaved Christian, concentrate on the happiness your loved one is experiencing right now with Jesus. Don't grieve in faithless despair. Wipe those tears from your eyes and rejoice!

> *When I have gone, remember I'm with Jesus;*
> *Then do not grieve because I've passed away;*
> *Life holds so many trials and disappointments,*
> *And will you weep because I did not stay?* —*Ryberg*

THOT: For the Christian, death is not SADNESS but GLADNESS.

THE COMFORT OF HIS COMING

... the dead in Christ shall rise first; then we ...
shall be caught up together with them. 1 Thessalonians 4:16,17

VISITORS to the Fiji Islands tell of a strange custom of "calling to the dead." The one who has suffered bereavement climbs to a high tree or a cliff, calls the name of the deceased, and then cries out pathetically, *"Come back! Come back!"* His heartrending wail is filled with despair, and only the mocking echoes underscore its sad frustration! Anyone who has recently lost a precious companion, a dear friend, or a beloved child can well appreciate the feeling of that forlorn figure. Just imagine the look upon his face, tears streaming down his cheeks, as he pitifully continues to plead for the return of his loved one.

Although Christians grieve when relatives are snatched from them by the pale specter of death, they sorrow not "as others who have no hope." Knowing that all who have died in the Lord will be raised incorruptible, they anticipate the return of Christ, the "Bright and Morning Star." Their longing cry is, *"Come back! Come back, Lord Jesus!"* They clearly recognize that on the glorious day of resurrection victory, those "who sleep in Jesus will God bring with Him." And this joyous event could happen at any moment. What a blessed reunion! What a clearing of tear-dimmed eyes when all the saints go marching in!

Are you eagerly awaiting that triumphant hour spoken of in 1 Thessalonians 4:17, when the trump of God shall sound and we shall be caught up "to meet the Lord in the air"? This promise of Scripture is not an idle hope, but a blessed certainty. Bereaved mourners, "comfort one another with these words."

> *Be still and trust, your flowing tears*
> *Will all be wiped away*
> *By God Himself, O grieving heart,*
> *Your Lord may come today.*   —Anon.

THOT: In the night of sorrow, only the trusting uplook can give the Christian a bright outlook!

LITTLE NELLIE

... lo, a great multitude ... stood before the throne,
... with ... palms in their hands. Revelation 7:9

HEAVEN is a place as real as New York or London! It is a realm of light and song where the saints of all ages fellowship with the risen Christ of Calvary. Do you believe this, or has it become a sort of "fairyland concept" for you?

In looking over my mother's keepsakes many years ago, I came across a folded piece of paper, yellowed with age. In childish handwriting were penciled the following tender words: "Our Nellie is with the angels now; she is waving a little palm branch in Heaven!" Nellie was Mother's 4-year-old sister who had always been sweet and thoughtful. She loved to speak of Jesus and Heaven, and especially enjoyed hearing about the saints who sing in Glory—robed in white and bearing palm branches in their hands. Mother told me that one weekend while grandfather was preaching in a distant city, Nellie became desperately ill with scarlet fever. The doctor was called but could do nothing to help her. With spiritual insight far beyond her years, Nellie said she was going to live with Jesus and would soon be waving "a little palm branch in Heaven." When the end came, the reality of the "many mansions" was impressed upon the hearts of everyone in the house. Mother, who was then 9 years old, loved her little sister very much and was deeply touched by her parting words. Finding a rainbow of hope in her tears, she went to her room and wrote the little note I discovered 72 years later!

Is Heaven real to you? I trust that through this story, little Nellie—though dead—"yet speaketh"!

There is a happy Land far, far away,
Where saints in Glory stand bright, bright as day;
O we shall happy be when from sin and sorrow free,
Lord, we shall dwell with Thee, blest, blest for aye!

— Young

THOT: The more you love Jesus, the more you long for Heaven.

I WON'T CRY AT MY FUNERAL!

God shall wipe away all tears.

Revelation 7:17

THE other night I had a very unusual dream. It was one of those dreams that seems so real you can hardly believe it didn't actually happen. I was at a funeral home and saw people weeping, including my closest relatives. I turned to a man who was wiping his eyes and inquired, "Who died?" He replied, "You must have known him—Henry Bosch of the Radio Bible Class!" At that moment I caught a glimpse of the figure in the casket. Sure enough, it was my body! Seeing my dear wife in deep sorrow, I choked up and began to cry.

Then suddenly I awoke. The dream was so vivid it kept me awake for a long while. I wiped the tears from my eyes and then began to smile. Why, *I'll never cry at my funeral,* I thought. I'll be rejoicing around God's throne—enjoying the pleasures of Heaven and fellowshiping with Jesus and my blessed loved ones who've gone before. Others may weep, but not me! Hallelujah! Just then my mood changed again to sadness as I remembered a personal friend who was dying from a serious illness. All his life he had rejected the gift of salvation, and unless he accepted the Lord soon, he would slip into a dreadful eternity without Jesus. I thought, *that poor lost soul will be crying when his funeral is held.* He will be in the darkness of that painful place where there is continuous weeping and wailing and gnashing of teeth.

O dear unsaved friend, accept the forgiveness and eternal life that the Savior freely offers to all who believe. Then by His grace you will never weep at your funeral!

> *I'll shed no tears, though some may weep*
> *When Heaven bids me to appear;*
> *For by His grace I'll shout with joy,*
> *"Thank God, there is no sorrow here!"* —Bosch

THOT: Those who truly fear God need not fear death.

THE AFTERGLOW

*Blessed are the dead who die in the Lord from henceforth.
. . . and their works do follow them.*   Revelation 14:13

OUR Christian deeds of love and testimony are like
stones cast into the pool of time. The ripples of their
influence extend on into eternity! The blind hymnwriter George Matheson exclaimed, "Thou has taught
me, O Lord, that our work need not end when our days
here come to a close; its impact can outlive the hands
that perform it. Indeed, much of the world's work is
done by those who have already departed, for we live
by the afterglow of the fruitful days they spent here.
When I see lives interrupted, I'm tempted to say, 'For
what purpose is this waste?' Help me, then, to remember that afterglow. For no force on earth is more
potent than that produced by those we call dead."

A child asked her mother, "Mommy, may I have one
of those little apple trees in the orchard?" "Why,
Mary, they're all yours. They belong to our family!"
"Yes, but I'd like to have one to call my very own.
Then I could give its apples as a present to the Lord."
When she was granted her wish, she ran to the orchard, laid her hand on a sapling, and said, "Little
tree, now you belong to Jesus." A few years later,
when the mother wrote to some missionaries, she
related that incident and concluded by saying, "Our
little girl was suddenly taken Home to be with the
Lord. She has been with Him in Heaven for many
months, and this year her tree bore fruit for the first
time. I'm enclosing the money we received from the
sale of those apples!"

Yes, Christians may "rest from their labors," but
their works follow them. When you die, will your influence continue to shed a wonderful afterglow?

> *When I have lived and bravely toiled,*
> *I'd like the world to find*
> *Some touch of truth and beauty here*
> *That I have left behind.*   —Anon.

THOT: A workman's best monument is the work he
has done.

123

THE FACE-TO-FACE MEETING
And they shall see His face.

Revelation 22:4

THIS wonderful promise in God's Word came to my mind when a friend sent me a copy of the delightful old gospel song, "The End of the Road." It was a favorite of my father, who is now in Glory. I recall one occasion when it was especially precious to him. He had suffered a severe heart attack and was unconscious. I had been trying to revive him, and when he came to, he stared at me almost sightlessly for a moment. Then he said with feeling, "Henry, someday I'll have a spell like this; and when I open my eyes, I won't see you, but *I'll look into my dear Savior's face!*" I knew he was thinking of the last stanza of that hymn he often sang around the house: "When I come to the end of the long, long road/ And trials will all be past,/ I'll look in the face of my dearest Friend,/ Safe home in His Heaven at last." What comfort and assurance those words brought to my father's heart!

Though the apostle Paul sometimes used the word "death," he also spoke of leaving this earth as "departing to be with Christ." He knew that the crowning joy of Heaven would be to meet and have fellowship with the Lord. O that we as Christians might truly appreciate the fact that Jesus is alive, that He is a real Man in the Glory, and that we shall someday behold Him in all His radiant loveliness.

Believer, are you looking forward to that time? I am! With tears of joy I write this meditation, and I echo with enthusiasm the words of that blessed old hymn, "When by His grace/ I shall look on His face,/ That will be glory for me!"

> Face to face I shall behold Him,
> Far beyond the starry sky;
> Face to face, in all His glory,
> I shall see Him by and by!   —Crosby

THOT: When in Heaven we view the sunshine of Christ's face, all earth's shadows will fall behind us.

6. God's Care and Providence

God cares for His children and is concerned with the most minute detail of their lives (Ps. 18:32). He is interested in things that we frequently consider too insignificant for Him to notice. But He knows how these so-called "little things" often influence important events and lead to serious consequences. His infinite knowledge and care extend even to the hairs of our head—indeed, each of them is numbered (Luke 12:7). We may then be confident that His all-wise providence is continually working out everything for our eternal good.

A Christian once toured a famous tapestry center in Paris to watch the skilled laborers perform their work of art. After observing for a while, he said to the supervisor, "I don't see any artistic value in that piece of work at all." He was told to return in a month and look at the finished product. Again all he saw were knots and a strange arrangement of colored threads. Then the director took him to the other side of the loom. What wondrous beauty, what skillful and artistic mingling of colors now met his eye! He learned that tapestry is woven from the wrong side. One who does not know what the weaver is doing sees only the tangled, snarled underside, not the exquisite design.

We too are being fashioned on the loom of life by the Master Weaver, who has all things in His power. His pattern of grace will be marvelous to behold when we see it from Heaven's clear perspective. There we will realize that the Lord has made our way "perfect."

Cheer up, Christian! With implicit faith in God's goodness, let Him have His way with you. If you do, your life will prove to be a Divine tapestry.

> *If He marks the sparrow's fall,*
> *Paints the lilies, short and tall,*
> *Gives the skies their azure hue,*
> *God will surely care for you!*   —*Anon.*

TRUST GOD IN THE DARK!

He knoweth the way that I take.

Job 23:10

THE believer in Christ can trust God even when he cannot trace Him. Like a good shepherd, the Lord will not fail to lead His own in safety. Though we may not understand our difficulty, we can be sure He knows the way, and He is guiding us in love to higher ground.

Job was a great saint, yet he had to endure what seemed to be unexplainable sorrow and suffering. And in Psalm 34:19, David says, "Many are the afflictions of the righteous; but the Lord delivereth him out of them all." God doesn't always show us why we must experience trials, but He assures us that they are sent for our good. The poet has written, "God knows the way, He holds the key,/ He guides us with unerring hand;/ Sometime with tearless eyes we'll see;/ Yes, there, up there, we'll understand."

A distressed farmer once said to a visiting Christian counselor, "It's hard for me to trust God when everything looks so dark." The man replied, "Well, brother, if you can't trust someone when he's out of your sight, he isn't worth much. So too, if you can't trust God in the dark, you really don't consider Him trustworthy." Then, pointing to a baby chicken that had just run over to its mother, he added, "See that little chick taking refuge under the hen's wing? Although it can't see anything there, it's still absolutely secure." Opening his Bible to Psalm 91, the counselor continued, "Notice, it doesn't say 'under His wings shalt thou *see,*' but 'under His wings shalt thou *trust.*'"

As children of God, we must face the problems of life with faith. Our Lord knows the way, so we can confidently trust Him in any circumstance.

There is a Guide that never falters,
And when He leads I cannot stray;
For step by step He goes before me
And marks my path—He knows the way.   —Ackley

THOT: The will of God will never lead you where the grace of God cannot keep you.

127

WHEN NELLIE "LEAPED OVER A WALL"

For by Thee I have run through a troop; and by my God have I leaped over a wall. Psalm 18:29

WHEN David spoke of jumping over an obstruction, he was using symbolic language. He implied that by trusting the Lord he could surmount every obstacle and be triumphant in the most depressing circumstances. That's what he meant when he said, " . . . *by my God* have I leaped over a wall."

My mother's sister Nellie was a woman of cheerful disposition and deep faith in God. For 5 years her husband had been ill in bed, completely incapacitated. In all that time she cared for him night and day until his death. The bills had mounted up, and she had no money to pay them. His insurance had lapsed, so the undertaker sympathetically agreed to wait for his fee. But through it all, Aunt Nellie was not depressed. When I visited her, she said, "God will supply my needs. I don't know how, but *He will!*" I marveled at her confidence in God's provision. A few days later she received some wonderful news. A piece of land in Texas purchased by her husband's father years before had produced a small amount of oil. Soon a letter arrived with a check for more than $5,000—her share of the earnings. It covered her expenses exactly—not a penny too little or too much. What joy flooded her soul! When she saw me again, she exclaimed with a radiant face, "Henry, isn't Jesus wonderful! He helped me in an unexpected way. By my God I have 'leaped over a wall.' "

Christian, let your heart be strengthened by this true story. The Lord specializes in solving problems that men think impossible. Take a leap of faith!

> *God's blessed Word reveals His care,*
> *On Him faith can depend;*
> *Beyond our every circumstance*
> *His promises extend!* —Adams

THOT: True faith sees the invisible, believes the incredible, and receives the impossible.

ACCIDENT OR INCIDENT?

The steps of a good man are ordered by the Lord.

Psalm 37:23

THE secret of Hudson Taylor's peace of mind in the midst of trouble was his refusal to look at secondary causes. As he labored on the mission field, he knew that his steps were ordered by the Lord and that nothing could happen without His all-wise approval. Referring to Job, Taylor remarked that even Satan had to get God's permission before he could afflict that righteous man with pain and sorrow. And although the adversary did bring about great calamities, Job was right in recognizing that his trials were ultimately a part of God's plan for his life. "To be sure," said Taylor, "the patriarch was deeply distressed and perplexed, but he never wavered in his confidence that the Lord's hand was upon him. He knew he was not the helpless victim of chance."

Rowland V. Bingham, founder of the Sudan Interior Mission, was injured in an automobile crash. His head was severely cut and a number of bones were broken. He was rushed to a hospital in critical condition. The following day he regained consciousness and asked the nurse what he was doing there. "Be very quiet," she replied. "You've been in a serious accident." "Accident?" said Bingham. "There are no accidents in the life of a Christian. This is just *an incident in God's perfect leading.*"

Have dark and difficult circumstances clouded your sky and obscured your pathway? Don't center your attention on secondary causes. Concentrate instead on the Lord, for He in wisdom is ordering your steps. Remember, *there are no accidents with Him!*

> *My Father's way may twist and turn,*
> *My heart may throb and ache,*
> *But in my soul I'm glad I know*
> *He maketh no mistake.* —*Overton*

THOT: If you think God makes mistakes, you're mistaken!

THE REWARD OF FAITH

. . . my soul trusteth in Thee. Yea, in the shadow of Thy
wings will I make my refuge.   Psalm 57:1

SOME time ago a story appeared in the *Covenant Companion* that brought blessing to my heart. A man named Cecil wanted to teach his little daughter the meaning of consecration and faith. So, taking her upon his knee in his library one day, he asked her if she loved him well enough to give up a little necklace of glass beads which she greatly prized. She looked up with tears in her eyes and said, "Yes, Papa." "Well," he said, "Then take them off and throw them into the fireplace." With a heavy heart and hesitating steps, she did as she was told, and then flew back to her father's arms sobbing. She finally became quiet when he patted her golden curls and gently said, "Now I know how much you love me."

Nothing more was said for several days. Then on her birthday her father called her, opened a small plush box, and handed her a chain of *real pearls!* He asked her to wear them as a gift of his love. As she looked into his eyes, the light of comprehension flooded her face. Again throwing herself into his arms, she cried, "O Papa! I didn't understand, but now I do!"

That's the kind of consecration God loves to honor. Our sacrifices are real investments that will bring us infinite returns in that day when He shall give us diadems for tears, cities for pounds, and multiplied interest on all that we have laid down for His sake.

Do not fret when God removes the baubles of time from your reluctant hands. Just believe that He is planning to replace them with the pearls of His eternal blessing. The rewards of faith are never disappointing.

> *Whate'er the crosses mine shall be,*
> *I would not dare to shun,*
> *But only ask to live for Thee,*
> *And that Thy will be done.*   —*Maxfield*

THOT: God's greatest blessings may come in rough
wrappings, but inside are golden benefits.

BUILD AGAIN—BUT HIGHER!

*I cry unto Thee, when my heart is overwhelmed; lead me
to the rock that is higher than I.*   Psalm 61:2

THIS plaintive cry was raised by the psalmist in a
time of trouble and discouragement. It may have been
when he was living a great distance from Jerusalem
and was in imminent danger from his enemies. He
had been in similar difficulty before, and had found
God to be a strong tower of protection. Once again he
needed a place of safety, and recognized that it had to
be on a lofty level. With a heart overwhelmed by the
prospect that was before him, he cried out to the Lord,
" . . . lead me to the rock that is higher than I." He
knew that God would give him a place of security far
beyond the reach of his menacing adversaries.

The psalmist's words reminded me of an incident
related by A. J. Gordon. He said if you tear down a
sparrow's nest, the little bird will build again in the
same place. However, if you pull it down several
times, she will seek a new location—a shelter higher
up—where it will be less vulnerable. Gordon then observed that Christians are not always so wise. They
form "dwelling places" of happiness and hope in this
temporal world, only to see them pulled down time
after time. Yet after each brief interval of sighs and
tears, they begin building all over again in the same
way. They never realize that through their defeats
the Lord is directing them to put their security in
Him—to set their sights heavenward. Gordon concluded his meditation with some good advice for every believer, whether assailed by men or chastened by God.
He said, "Christians should learn to imitate the sparrow who builds her nest again— *but higher!*"

> *My heart has no desire to stay*
> *Where doubts arise and fears dismay;*
> *Though some may dwell where these abound,*
> *My prayer, my aim, is higher ground.—Oatman*

THOT: The best way to live in the world is to live
above it.

GOD'S PINIONS: A SAFE RETREAT

*He shall cover thee with His feathers, and under His
wings shalt thou trust.* Psalm 91:4

SOME of the best sermons are those that are seen
rather than heard. A preacher made the following observation which preaches a splendid sermon: "While
in the country, I sat watching a brood of chicks in a
farmyard as they were all pecking away beside their
mother. The big hen was cluck—cluck—clucking, as
only she could. All the while she was scratching for
food, the little ones were following her example. Suddenly a strange dog leaped over the fence and ad-
vanced toward the chickens. My, didn't that mother
hen look fierce when she saw him! The dog was actually frightened by her actions. Meanwhile, the little
chicks had run to her and were peeping out from their
places of safety beneath her wings with a defiant and
impudent look, as if to say: 'Ah! you big black dog,
you won't get us here!' They didn't come out but were
secure in the refuge that God had given them—the
warm, sheltering pinions of their mother. I thought to
myself, there is a spiritual lesson here. If you belong
to Jesus, the 'big black dog of Hell' can't touch you.
Close to the Lord, you are sheltered from all harm."
Oh the gentle, keeping power of God; the warmth of
His breast, the security of His "pinions of providence"!

As you read the entire 91st Psalm, you recognize
that the wings referred to are those of the "cherubim"
in the holy place. Yes, God's angels form a "hedge"
about His own when they dwell in the "secret place"
of full consecration (Job 1:10; Ps. 34:7). With such a
holy band guarding us, we find in Christ a safe retreat
for time and eternity!

Under His wings I am safely abiding,
Though the night deepens and tempests are wild;
Still I can trust Him—I know He will keep me,
He has redeemed me and I am His child. —Cushing

THOT: For the Christian, what appears to be the
dark snare of trouble is only the shadow of
God's wing!

"GOD WILL TAKE CARE OF YOU"

Then they cried unto the Lord in their trouble, and He
saved them out of their distresses.   Psalm 107:13

COMMENTING on this text, J. C. Philpott observed, "Note that they cried unto the Lord *in* their trouble. Not before nor after, but *in it!*" The verse concludes with the assuring statement that "He saved them out of their distresses."

Pastor W. S. Martin found himself in a perplexing situation. He was scheduled to preach in a distant village, yet he was worried about leaving home because his wife had unexpectedly become ill. After pondering and praying about his problem, he mentioned it to his young son. Undoubtedly led by the Lord, the boy gave the advice he needed. "Don't be afraid to go, Dad. I'm sure God will take good care of Mother while you're away." The pastor remembered how he had often impressed upon his son that he should put the Lord first in his life, and that he should keep his commitments whenever possible. So, casting aside his anxiety, he went in the confidence of Psalm 37:23, believing that the Lord was ordering his steps. The services were richly blessed by God, and when he returned home, his wife was much improved. To express her gratitude to the Lord, she had written a poem about His loving help and providential care. Within an hour, Pastor Martin improvised a melody on the organ to fit the words. It has become a famous and much-loved hymn: "Be not dismayed whate'er betide,/ God will take care of you;/ Beneath His wings of love abide,/ God will take care of you."

Troubled believer, the Lord is interested in you and your problems. Call upon Him and He will direct your steps. He'll graciously take care of you.

> *Through days of toil when heart doth fail,*
> *God will take care of you;*
> *When dangers fierce your path assail,*
> *God will take care of you.*   — Martin

THOT: Roll your burden on the Lord—if you do the CASTING, He'll do the CARING.

"JESUS AND I"

I will strengthen thee; yea, I will help thee. Isaiah 41:10
I am with you always.   Matthew 28:20

WE all need the strength of the Lord to sustain us, especially when an unknown fear grips our hearts. Christ has promised to be near us at all times in the person of the Holy Spirit. The Scriptures assure us that we can always depend on Him to help and uphold us.

The *Christian Herald* had an article about Dan Crawford that underscores this truth. He had the difficult task of following in the steps of David Livingstone, the missionary who gave his life in ministering the Word of God to Africa. Crawford didn't have the imposing personality of his famous predecessor, so at first he had trouble winning the loyalty of the tribal people. Even his church back home wasn't sure he could carry on the work. With God's help, however, he did a magnificent job. When he died, a well-worn copy of the New Testament was found in his pocket. A poem handwritten on the inside cover, evidently his own, revealed the secret of his success: "I cannot do it alone!/ The waves dash fast and high;/ The fog comes chilling around,/ And the light goes out in the sky./ But I know that we two shall win in the end—/ Jesus and I./ Coward, and wayward, and weak,/ I change with the changing sky,/ Today so strong and brave,/ Tomorrow too weak to fly;/ but HE never gives in! So we two shall win/ Jesus and I!"

As you encounter a new task or face the demands of your trials, your dependence on the Lord will make all the difference. Because He is there to strengthen and comfort, you can say, "I know that we two shall win in the end—*Jesus and I!*"

> *When in the midst of life with its problems,*
> *Bent with our toil and burdens we bear,*
> *Wonderful thought and deep consolation:*
> *Jesus is always there!*   —*Lillenas*

THOT: It is not just the sense of His presence but the fact of His presence that is our strength.

CARRIED BY GOD

In all their affliction He was afflicted, . . . in His love
. . . He bore them, and carried them.   Isaiah 63:9

THE Lord knows all about our griefs and troubles, and He is deeply touched by them. The prophet said of God and His people, "In all their affliction He was afflicted." When Jesus was on earth, His loving heart was filled with compassion for needy individuals. Still today He sustains His own in times of crisis.

An unknown author has recorded this comforting and enlightening story: "One night I dreamed I was walking along the beach with the Lord. Many scenes from my life flashed before me. In each one I noticed footprints in the sand. Sometimes there were two sets, but at other times there was only one. This bothered me because I noted that during periods of depression, when I was suffering from anguish, sorrow, or severe testing, I could see only a single set. So I prayed in my distress, 'You promised, Lord, that if I followed You, You'd walk with me always. But I've noticed that during the most trying period of my life, there has been just one set of prints in the sand. Why, when I needed You most, haven't You been with me?' To which the Lord replied, 'The times when only ONE set of footprints were made, My child, were the times I CARRIED you!' "

Yes, believer, in your moments of crisis the Good Shepherd will bear you up in His everlasting arms (Dt. 33:27). No matter how deep the waters of trouble may be, God's promise is sure: " . . . they shall not overflow thee" (Isa. 43:2). He'll carry you through the rising current and bring you safely to the high plateau of His comforting peace and sheltering love.

> *God the Eternal is your refuge,*
> *Let Him still your wild alarms;*
> *Underneath your deepest sorrow*
> *Are His everlasting arms.*   —Simpson

THOT: God never sends a heavy burden to weigh us down without offering His mighty arm to lift us up.

135

WHY FLETCHER MISSED THE BOAT

... it is not in man ... to direct his steps.   Jeremiah 10:23
The steps of a good man are ordered by the Lord. Psalm 37:23

A YOUNG man named John Fletcher was always looking for a new adventure. One day he met a mariner who told strange tales of a little-known country called Brazil, where pots full of gold were supposedly stored in caves just waiting for the taking. Fletcher decided to go there on a ship being outfitted at a local port. The next morning he ordered a servant to bring him a steaming kettle of water for his usual cup of tea. Somehow it tipped from the table, and its boiling contents scalded him severely. Unable to move when the ship left port, he cursed the fate that had confined him to his room with an injured leg. Looking out the window, he watched the sails of the boat disappear over the horizon. He little knew that God was graciously sparing his life, for the ship was never heard of again. Later, Fletcher was wonderfully converted and became an associate of John Wesley. His biographer says, "He then became a soul-adventurer going into distant lands of spiritual conquest. He also devoted his attention to training men for the ministry; and the books he wrote on the Bible became classics." John Fletcher, who wanted to find gold, missed the boat because God had greater treasures for him.

Your so-called missed opportunities and your unexpected disappointments may well be the Lord's way of leading you into greener pastures of activity. Daily ask the Savior to direct your steps along the pathway of His highest will for your life, and then obediently follow Him. Never doubt that He will bring you to the highlands of full blessing and spiritual usefulness.

> *Where He may lead me I will go,*
> *For I have learned to trust Him so;*
> *His divine will is sweet to me,*
> *Hallowed by blood-stained Calvary.*   *—Martin*

THOT: Many a life that seems MARRED by accident is only in the process of being MADE by providence.

HE GOES BEFORE!

*And when He putteth forth His own sheep, He goeth
before them, and the sheep follow Him.*   John 10:4

BECAUSE we are weak, helpless sheep, not wise
enough to find our own way, we need to trust our lives
to the unerring guidance of the Good Shepherd. He
searches out the safe path for us, and what is more,
He goes on ahead! As someone has so beautifully remarked, *"Christ is in all the tomorrows that we will
have to journey through.* We may be sure, therefore,
that all is safe farther ahead where He is leading." O
that we might exclaim with the poet, "Keep Thou my
feet; I do not ask to see the distant scene — *one step
enough for me!"*

As His trusting sheep, we have one thing to do:
FOLLOW HIM! He never stumbles, never wavers in
His perfect guidance. "Then wherefore should I doubt
my Shepherd's voice, or falter more? Not mine to
choose the path, but mine to know He goes before!"

A missionary had to pass through some unfamiliar
territory in the middle of the night. As he went
through the darkness with his guide going on ahead,
he looked down and could see no road. The guide
turned so frequently that the missionary feared the
way had been missed. In his anxiety he finally cried,
"Where is the way?" The native who was leading
turned around and said, *"I am the way.* There is no
beaten path here; just follow me step by step, and you
will reach the end of the journey safely." The missionary did as he was told and soon arrived at his destination. Today let us concentrate less upon the obscure
road we are asked to tread, and fix our eyes upon our
Guide, who is THE WAY, and by faith follow Him!

> *I was not ever thus, nor prayed that Thou*
> *Shouldst lead me on;*
> *I loved to choose and see my path;*
> *But now — lead Thou me on!*   —*Newman*

THOT: The hidden things of God are not discovered
until we are treading the path of absolute
obedience!

NEVER DOUBT GOD'S GOODNESS!

He that spared not His own Son, . . . how shall He not
with Him also freely give us all things?   Romans 8:32

THE *Sunday School Times* carried the story of a man in Dundee, Scotland, who had fallen and broken his back as a lad of 15. For 40 years he was confined to his bed and could move only with great difficulty. A day never passed that he didn't suffer excruciating pain. But he was a fine Christian and found God's grace sufficient for all his needs. Many came to see him because his cheery disposition and great love for the Lord filled their own hearts with new courage. One day a friend asked, "Doesn't the devil ever tempt you to doubt God?" "Yes, he tries to make me question His providence. It's hard to lie here and see my old schoolmates drive by in their cars, having a good time with their families. At times Satan whispers, 'If the Lord is so good, why does He keep you here? Why did He permit you to break your back?' " The visitor then inquired, "What do you do when the devil sows those seeds of discontent?" The victorious invalid exclaimed, "I've found a wonderful way to deal with him. I point him to Calvary, and show him the wounds of my Savior. Then I say to him, *'Doesn't He love me!'* He can't answer that, so he flees every time."

That bedridden saint was so full of faith in God that he did not complain. He knew that the One who gave His only begotten Son to save him certainly wouldn't grieve him needlessly. The same love that sent Christ to Calvary was still working for his good in all of life's problems.

Christian, you can blame sin and Satan for some of the things you can't understand, but don't ever doubt the goodness of God!

> *I will not doubt, though all my ships at sea*
> *Come drifting home with broken masts and sails;*
> *I shall believe the Hand which never fails,*
> *For seeming evil worketh good for me.*   — *Wilcox*

THOT: Faith glorifies God, but doubt delights the devil.

"GRACE" FOR "THEE"!

My grace is sufficient for thee.

2 Corinthians 12:9

IN a sermon preached over radio station WMBI some years ago, E. W. Palmer made an observation about this verse which proved a blessing to thousands. This was especially true because he delivered that message shortly after the accidental death of his wife and his 16-year-old son. Palmer said, "I have discovered in my experience in the ministry that people find it difficult to appropriate God's grace. That is, they do not apply it to themselves, to make it their very own. I recall walking into a meeting where Dr. Walter Wilson was speaking. He greeted me by saying, 'How is it now, beloved?' Although grief-stricken, I replied, 'Oh, His grace is sufficient.' Wilson shook his head, 'Say that again,' he suggested. I repeated, 'My grace is sufficient.' He said, 'Say it again.' This time I replied, 'My grace is sufficient for thee.' His comment was, 'You know, Pastor, you left out the best part the first few times you quoted that blessed Scripture. When you put the "thee" in there, you make it your own.' " Then Palmer concluded, "In general terms we frequently say, God's grace is sufficient; and that is true. But the question is, Have we appropriated it and made it our very own? Whatever I get through grace I do not deserve. However, I have access to it because of His goodness to me; but *it is my duty to receive it and make it my own!*"

God's grace is sufficient for all your difficulties. It will carry you through any emergency if you will look to Christ in faith and then personally appropriate His abundant supply of unfailing comfort.

He giveth more grace when the burdens grow greater;
He sendeth more strength when the labors increase.
To added affliction He addeth His mercy;
To multiplied trials, His multiplied peace. —*Flint*

THOT: The increasing darkness of trial only makes the lamp of grace shine brighter.

A HAT CHANGED TWO LIVES

... the things which happened ... have fallen out rather
unto the furtherance of the gospel.   Philippians 1:12

THE apostle Paul had the right attitude toward suffering. He made many sacrifices to preach the good news of Jesus' love. He gave up his business, left his friends, and suffered beatings, stonings, shipwreck, hunger, and imprisonment. He even had an affliction which he called "a thorn in the flesh." But Paul did not complain about his difficulties; instead he saw the good in them. He wrote, "But I would ye should understand, brethren, that the things which happened unto me have fallen out rather unto the furtherance of the gospel."

Richard Storrs and Gordon Hall were students together at the same theological seminary. One Saturday toward the end of the semester, Hall prepared to go to Braintree, Massachusetts, to preach. He hoped that he might receive the invitation to become their pastor. That afternoon as he was splitting some wood, his hat fell beneath the ax and was ruined. He didn't have the money to replace it, and the weather was bitter cold, so he asked his friend to take his assignment for him. Storrs preached and later accepted the call to be the minister of that parish, where he remained until his dying day—a period of more than half a century! Although Hall was disappointed, he sought other outlets for his talents and became a renowned foreign missionary. No one who believes in Divine providence will doubt for one moment that God sent Storrs to Braintree and Hall to the mission field. The courses of two lives were changed by means of that ruined hat, and it worked "unto the furtherance of the gospel."

Go on with God, all things shall work for good,
E'en all the things that are not understood;
The seed you're sowing in the gospel field,
Mingled with tears, shall bring a glorious yield. —Anon.

THOT: There are no accidents with God—only incidents with a divine purpose!

"HERE COMES THE LORD'S ANSWER!"

God shall supply all your need according to His riches
in glory by Christ Jesus. Philippians 4:19

WHEN Christians encounter trouble, they should claim God's promises and prayerfully bring their problems to His attention. Although the Lord is fully aware of each need, He is pleased when His children acknowledge their complete dependence on Him and seek His help.

A preacher was returning home one Saturday afternoon after a week of exhausting activity. Suddenly he felt the Holy Spirit prompting him to visit a poor widow who lived with her invalid daughter on the outskirts of town. At first he was inclined to dismiss the thought from his mind, but a strong feeling of urgency persisted. So he turned around and headed back toward her small cottage. He was thinking only of the widow's spiritual needs, but when he arrived at her home he was struck once more with her dire poverty. Putting some money in her hand, he inquired how they were doing. When he learned that she and her daughter had been without food since the night before, he asked what she had done about her problem. "I just laid everything before the Savior in prayer!" she answered. "Did you talk about your need to anyone else?" questioned the pastor. "Oh, no! No one knew about it but God and me. I knew He wouldn't forget us, even though I wasn't sure just what He'd do. Then I saw you stop out front, and I said to myself, 'Hallelujah, *here comes the Lord's answer!*' "

By faith bring all your pressing needs to your Heavenly Father (Phil. 4:19). He'll hear and answer in His own wonderful way.

> *His blessed Word reveals His care,*
> *On Him you can depend;*
> *Beyond each needy circumstance*
> *His promises extend.* —Adams, alt.

THOT: Man's poverty never strains God's provision.

JESUS IS ALL YOU NEED!

For in that He Himself hath suffered being tempted,
He is able to help them that are tempted. Hebrews 2:18

THE Lord Jesus is ever mindful of His children, and He has promised to help them in time of trouble. Because He victoriously endured the most severe testings that could be brought upon any man, He understands what Christians feel, and He can satisfy their deep spiritual longings.

A saint of God who had experienced the Savior's gracious care through adversity wrote these words of testimony: "Am I wounded? Christ is balm. Am I sick? He is medicine. Am I poor? He is wealth. Am I hungry? He is bread. Am I thirsty? He is water. Am I in debt? He is my surety. Am I in darkness? He is my sun and shield. Must I face black clouds and a gathering storm? He is an anchor both sure and steadfast. Am I being tried? He pleads for me as my perfect advocate. *In every human need, Christ is my all!*"

An elderly preacher said that as a boy he used to see so many people draw water from the old-fashioned village well that he was afraid it would run dry. To find out if the supply really was running out, he descended the steps of the well one morning and marked the water level. Checking back that night, he found as much water as before, even though people had been drawing from it all day. A perennial spring was constantly replenishing the supply. From that early experience the preacher drew this application: Christ is the inexhaustible wellspring of grace, who is able to meet every need of every believer.

Christian, in your hours of distress, look to the Savior. By faith you will receive His sympathetic help and refreshment. Jesus is all you need!

> *All that I need He will always be,*
> *All that I need till His face I see;*
> *All that I need through eternity,*
> *Jesus is all I need.* —Rowe

THOT: Christ does not always take us out of trials, but He does take us through them.

PROPER CASTING

Cast not away, therefore, your confidence.   Hebrews 10:35
Casting all your care upon Him.   1 Peter 5:7

THE way a child of God reacts under pressure is the true test of his spiritual stature. This text gives us specific guidance in facing trying situations. One thing we should never do is lose faith and confidence in the goodness of God and the rightness of His leading. Instead, we are to cast every care upon our loving Savior, the Lord Jesus Christ, and find peace by leaving our burdens with Him.

When I was a boy, my mother was deeply concerned about my future. Although I had survived two bouts with tuberculosis, I had been left weak and crippled. When she privately expressed her anxiety to an acquaintance, he gave her good advice. "Mrs. Bosch," he said, "you must stop worrying about your boy and cast all your care upon the Lord. I am sure He has the answer to all these problems. Somehow He will make it possible for Henry to support himself when you and your husband are gone." How right that dear brother was! Gradually my body grew stronger, I was able to go on to college, get into gospel broadcasting, and finally work at the Radio Bible Class. Not only did I take care of my own needs, but after my father's death I provided for my mother, my wife, and three adopted children. Then Mother realized that although her loving concern for her son had been a natural one, it was a needless worry. Instead of casting away her confidence, she should have followed the admonition in 1 Peter 5:7 and cast her care upon the Lord.

Remember, Christian, in times of trial you can have victory if you do the proper kind of casting!

Our Heavenly Father bids us cast our care on Him
   each day;
He also bids us not to cast our confidence away;
But oh, how foolishly we act when taken unawares!
We cast away our confidence and carry all our cares!

THOT: Our work is to CAST CARE; God's work is to
          TAKE CARE!

GOD'S INEXHAUSTIBLE GRACE

*But the God of all grace, . . . after ye have suffered awhile,
make you perfect, . . . strengthen, settle you.* 1 Peter 5:10

IN our text the Father in Heaven is referred to as "the God of *all grace.*" He has justifying grace for the believer, illuminating grace for the seeker, comforting grace for the bereaved, and strengthening grace for the weak. He also has sanctifying grace for the unholy, living grace for the Christian pilgrim, and dying grace for His world-weary child as he comes to the end of life's journey. Without question, His grace is sufficient for every need.

In an extinct volcano on the island of Trinidad is a crater that is completely filled with pitch. Although gas escapes from below, forming bubbles here and there, the surface is firm enough for people to walk on. For several decades, huge loads of asphalt have been dug from this tar-like lake and shipped to all parts of the world for use in paving roads. I am told that no matter how large a hole is made when removing pitch from the crater, it doesn't remain more than 72 hours because it fills up from below. Shiploads of asphalt have been taken out of this crater for almost 75 years, yet it never runs empty. Drillings reveal that this black, gum-like substance is still found at a depth of 280 feet. The supply seems to be endless. In a small way, this pictures God's infinite grace which never diminishes. *No matter how great our problems, His love is never exhausted!*

Believer, your situation may be extremely difficult, but His marvelous grace is sufficient to give you the peace and the security you so desperately need.

> *His love has no limit, His grace has no measure,*
>   *His power has no boundary known unto men;*
> *For out of His infinite riches in Jesus,*
>   *He giveth, and giveth, and giveth again!*   —*Flint*

THOT: Grace is God's infinite love expressing itself in infinite goodness.

144

7. Loneliness and Old Age

Time is swiftly passing, but this should not alarm the aging Christian. He is not headed for the sunset but *for the sunrise* of Glory! At 90 years of age, Henry Burton wrote, "I sit by my western window and think of the long ago,/ When the eastern hills were lightened in the morning's rosy glow;/ Bright were the hours of the morning, and brighter the hour of noon,/ But better still is the gloaming, for *the best is coming soon!*"

Physicians will confirm that people with true faith in God, and the will to live happily, have a much better rate of survival than those who are gloomy and depressed. A heart made "merry" by the grace of God is indeed a splendid "medicine" (Prov. 17:22).

Former President James A. Garfield once remarked, "If wrinkles must be written upon our brows, never let them be written upon our hearts, for our spirit must never grow old!" The idea that we must lie down and die because we are getting elderly is foolish. Who is old? Not the man of spiritual energy but the one who allows his powers to waste away through pessimism and defeat. The years God gives us are just enough for the work He allots us. So let's "redeem the time." If we do, we'll have a "continual feast" (Prov. 15:15).

145

Though we may slow down or cease to participate in certain activities, there are always new vistas for praying and witnessing that are open to the aging believer. We must keep looking ahead, for dedication to Christ is for life (Lk. 9:62). Determine then to *go forward*—cost what it may; God has provided *no armor for the Christian's back*. With the courage of the unknown poet, let's make his words our prayer.

Keep me from turning back;
Ne'er let the reins be slack;
  The handles of my plow with tears are wet,
  The cutting shears with rust are spoiled; and yet—
My God! My God! Keep me from turning back!

THE PEPPY "CALEB" GENERATION

I am as strong . . . as I was in the day that Moses sent me.
Now, therefore, give me this mountain. Joshua 14:11,12

A RECENT issue of *New Horizons* reported some surprising statistics. Elderly people are not as different as we have been led to believe. Because some of them reside in rest homes or must be in hospitals, we conclude that they represent all who are rounding out their "threescore years and ten." The National Council on Aging hired the Harris polling organization to interview 1500 individuals under 65 and another 2500 past that age. The younger ones thought that the older people sit around and sleep a lot, that loneliness and poor health are their most serious problems, and that they have trouble keeping busy. The response of the other group, however, indicated that these conditions apply only to the minority. While 31 percent of those over 65 are inactive, just 12 percent complain of loneliness. While 56 percent of the younger thought that the elderly were disturbed by "not feeling needed," this was true of only 7 percent of the senior citizens. In fact, most of them reported that they had plenty to do and were still functioning well.

In Joshua 14 we read that Caleb was strong and vigorous even at 85, and that he asked for a challenging assignment. His cry was not for the easy places of retirement, but rather, *"Give me this mountain."* Not everyone who is elderly is spiritually empowered like that godly leader of Israel; but one thing is sure—we must not look down on those in the upper-age bracket as if all of them were weak and incompetent. The Harris Poll seems to indicate that many are still healthy and active. So don't underestimate the peppy "Caleb" generation!

> *It is not age that makes us old—*
> *The spirit may be young,*
> *Though more than threescore years and ten*
> *The wheels of life have run!* —Anon.

THOT: Youth is not only a time of life, it's a state of mind!

SITTING OUT THE CONCERT

And he requested for himself that he might die,
and said, It is enough!   1 Kings 19:4

THE concert is in full swing. The conductor is waving his baton with zeal and enthusiasm. Suddenly a member of the orchestra approaches him. It's the man who plays the triangle. He bends over and whispers, "Do you mind, sir, if I go home now? I have come to the end of my part of the score." How ridiculous! you say. Even if he can only function in a minor capacity, he still is a member of the musical group and is expected to "sit out the concert." Just his presence adds a certain touch. Without him the orchestra will not look its best. The work of the others would be disturbed and disrupted if some were to leave the moment they thought their main contribution to the program had been made.

Some senior citizens feel useless, and others are dwelling under the "juniper tree of self-pity" like Elijah, wishing that God would say, "It is enough!" They believe they've already given their performance. Whether they know it or not, however, they are significantly adding to the "orchestra of life" by just being there. Many younger people, observing these elderly saints, have been impressed by their patience, their wisdom, and their rich prayer-life. Consequently, they are blessed by their influence. What the full impact of their spiritual efforts will be, only eternity will reveal. They have much to accomplish for God's glory, even as Elijah, and they are very important. Otherwise God wouldn't leave them here on earth.

Elderly Christian, even though your major task here may have been completed, you are still making a worthwhile contribution by "sitting out the concert."

> *Lord, help me be a blessing still*
> *To family and to friend;*
> *That I may serve some purpose true*
> *Until my life shall end.*   —Bosch

THOT: You are young and useful at any age if you are still planning for tomorrow!

148

THE FLOWER CLOCK

My days are swifter than a weaver's shuttle.

Job 7:6

YEAR after year we become increasingly aware that the older generation is vanishing from the arena of activity. As we ponder the ceaseless current that bears us onward to eternity, we are impressed with what seems to be an accelerating passage of time. Job compared the rapid movement of his days to the lightning-like movements of the "weaver's shuttle." The relentless flow of the years need not alarm the Christian, however, for the Scriptures assure us that God's grace is adequate for every need and that His hand will guide unerringly to Glory (Ps. 73:24).

History records that the noted botanist Linnaeus once devised a clock with a face of flowers. Each of the buds opened in turn at a set time of the day. God has a similar order and beauty in the garden of life. Carefully, steadily He unfolds the petals of time before us, so that we may extract from them the nectar of His mercy and the honey of His never-failing blessings. Realizing that "the path of the just is like the shining light, that shineth more and more unto the perfect day" (Prov. 4:18), we should never be pessimistic about the Lord's dealings with us. The Bible reveals that His will for us is always kind. We may be sure that the buds which circle the clock of time will open in beauty at their appointed hour, and that each moment He'll give sufficient strength to face all our problems.

Although the years roll swiftly by, let's not measure the days by "the water clock" of our falling tears, but by "the flower clock" of God's guidance and grace.

> *Now is the only time you own,*
> *So trust and toil with a will;*
> *Place your faith in the love of God,*
> *Till the clock of life is still.* —McCartney

THOT: Don't count the passing days—just make the passing days count.

BRINGING BLESSINGS TO THE AGED

Cast me not off in the time of old age; forsake me
not when my strength faileth.   Psalm 71:9

SOME people dread old age because they fear that it may involve loneliness, physical decline, and giving up many enjoyable activities. When the psalmist was young, he said with confidence, "For the Lord . . . forsaketh not His saints" (Ps. 37:28). As the glow of youth began to fade, however, he prayed in a moment of discouragement, "Cast me not off in the time of old age; forsake me not when my strength faileth."

Many elderly Christians have days when their faith is weak, and they need special consideration from others to undergird and cheer them. Esther M. Walker has expressed this truth in a poem entitled, "Beatitudes for Friends of the Aged." Slightly altered, it reads:

> Blessed are they who understand
> My faltering step and my palsied hand.
> Blessed are they who know today
> My ears must strain to catch what they say.
> Blessed are they who never say,
> "You've told that story three times today."
> Blessed are they who know the ways
> To bring back memories of yesterdays.
> Blessed are they with cheery smile
> Who've stopped on their way to chat a while.
> Blessed are they who ease the days
> On my journey Home with loving ways!

Christian, how long has it been since you did a kind deed for some senior citizen, or visited a rest home to bring blessing to one of God's saints?

> *Lord, teach me how to love and live,*
> *That I may cheer some heart,*
> *And to the elderly in need*
> *Some comfort thus impart.*   —Anon.

THOT: Showing kindness to the aged helps soften the lengthening shadows of their sunset years.

OUR MEASURED TIME

So teach us to number our days, that we may apply
our hearts unto wisdom.   Psalm 90:12

THE expression translated "number" in our text comes from a root word meaning "to weigh" or "to measure." We are to place each day in the balance and make our lives tip the scales in a way that will bring glory to God and blessing to others. It has been said, "It's not *how long* we live that is important, but *how well* we live!" If we realize the value of our days and spend them profitably, the years will take care of themselves. A rich harvest, both now and in the life to come, will result from daily applying "our hearts unto wisdom."

A. C. Dixon said that when the brilliant Raphael died at the age of 37, some of his friends and relatives carried his marvelous painting "The Transfiguration" in the funeral procession. It was only partially finished, and because of his youth and the limited time he was allotted to use his creative genius, they felt it was a symbol of his unfulfilled earthly aspirations. But actually that half-completed picture has a deeper meaning—a message that should impress itself upon all of us: life's sojourn is fleeting and death sometimes terminates even our best efforts. Since we have no guarantee of tomorrow, we should treasure each hour as a jewel of great value and use it to the best advantage.

To have no regrets but much reward in Heaven, we must "walk circumspectly, not as fools but as wise, *redeeming the time*" (Eph. 5:15,16). With the psalmist, therefore, let us pray, "Lord, make me to know mine end, and the *measure of my days*" (Ps. 39:4).

> *The clock of life is wound but once,*
> *And no man has the power*
> *To tell just when the hands will stop,*
> *At late or early hour!*   —Anon.

THOT: Don't just mark time, use time to make your mark!

151

BEAUTIFIED BY GRACE

And let the beauty of the Lord our God be upon us.

Psalm 90:17

WITH the brush of His creative hand, God paints the flowers of the field, colors the evening sky with the beautiful hues of ebbing day, and gives to nature a breathtaking loveliness. Indeed, He is the fountain and source of all beauty. Meditating on this truth, the writer of Psalm 90 prayed that grace would overrule Israel's iniquity so they could radiate some of the glory of their Maker. His earnest plea is summed up in the words, "And let the beauty of the Lord our God be upon us."

The psalmist's desire should be the goal of every child of God, but some never achieve it. Instead of growing in grace, they lose the glow of spirituality. As time passes, they become more and more crotchety. Their witness fades and is no longer effective. Their dour faces betray a broken spirit. Other Christians, however, learn to trust and praise the Lord at all times, and their personalities exhibit the pleasantness of a truly sanctified life.

An American traveling in India was greatly impressed by the dignity and charm of an elderly, white-haired lady. She was a saint of God who had acquired the shining quality of spiritual maturity. "Ma'am," he said as he looked at her wrinkled but smiling face, "believe me, you are truly beautiful!" "Well, I ought to be," she replied sweetly, *"I've had 74 years to let the Lord work on me!"*

Does your life convey a message of holy joy? As you live by faith on the victory side of trial and hardship, the beauty of the Lord will increasingly radiate from your countenance!

> *Dear Jesus, take my heart and hand,*
> *And grant me this I pray:*
> *That I through Your sweet love may grow*
> *More like You day by day.* —Garrison

THOT: Graceful and honorable old age is the childhood of immortality.

A FRUITFUL OLD AGE

They shall still bring forth fruit in old age.

WE cannot keep from growing old, but by the grace of God we can avoid the pitfalls that make some elderly folks peevish and unfruitful. When Longfellow was quite aged, an admirer asked how he was able to remain vigorous and write so beautifully. Pointing to an apple tree, the poet replied, "That tree has been there a long time, but I never saw prettier flowers on it than those it has right now. Its branches display a little new wood each year, and I suppose that is what accounts for the lovely blossoms. Like that tree, *I still grow new wood each year!*" We can't stop time, but we can keep growing and bearing spiritual fruit.

The following prayer for the elderly is worth repeating: "Lord, Thou knowest I am growing older. Keep me from the idea that I must express myself on every subject. Release me from the craving to meddle in everyone's affairs. Keep my tongue from the recital of endless details of the past which do not interest others. Seal my lips when I am inclined to talk about my aches and pains. They are increasing with the years, and my love to speak of them grows sweeter as time goes by. Teach me the glorious lesson that occasionally I may be wrong. Make me thoughtful, but not interfering; helpful, but not bossy. With the wisdom and experience I've gained, it does seem a pity not to use it all, but Thou knowest, Lord, that I want a few friends left at the end. So help me to pray more, talk less. And beyond all this, let me continue to flourish spiritually and bring forth fruit to Thy glory even in old age. Amen!"

Let me grow lovely growing old as many fine things do,
For silks and ivory and gold need not be always new;
And there is healing in old trees, old streets a glamour hold,
So why not I, as well as they, grow lovely growing old?

—Anon.

THOT: To stay youthful, keep useful!

"IT IS TOWARD EVENING"

*Abide with us; for it is toward evening.... And [Jesus]
went in to tarry with them.* Luke 24:29

TIME keeps rolling on. The more we leave youth behind, the faster the days seem to slip away. For many, the high noon of their time here on earth has passed. The shadows of advancing years begin to lengthen across the autumn landscape of their lives. As I was reading Luke 24, I was reminded that for many it is *"toward evening."* When the outward man is beginning to perish, how blest we are if we can say, " . . . yet the inward man is renewed day by day" (2 Cor. 4:16).

One who was closely associated with Andrew Bonar of Glasgow frequently repeated the sentiments expressed by Bonar's father. "Andrew," he would often say, "pray that we both may *wear well to the end!*" Wasn't this also the earnest desire of the apostle Paul? Disregarding the chains which bound him, and discounting his many afflictions, he victoriously declared, "But none of these things move me . . . that I might finish my course with joy" (Acts 20:24). The life of the indwelling Christ kept Paul tranquil, hopeful, and happy to the very end. The Savior can do the same for us.

Some years ago a saintly man of God said on his 95th birthday, "I am still at work—with my hand to the plow and my face to the future. The shadows of evening lengthen about me, but morning is in my heart!" This can be the testimony of God's children everywhere who have Christ reigning within.

Elderly saints can offer no better prayer than the words directed to Jesus by the disciples on the Emmaus road: *"Abide with us; for it is toward evening."*

Swift to its close ebbs out life's little day,
Earth's joys grow dim, its glories pass away;
Change and decay in all around I see—
O Thou who changest not, abide with me! —*Lyte*

THOT: For the Christian, old age is the forerunner of eternal youth.

154

"HE DIED CLIMBING"

*I press toward the mark for the prize of the high
calling of God in Christ Jesus.* Philippians 3:14

ONE of the most disturbing things in the world is to
see elderly people who have lost all incentive to live.
They either look back constantly with regret and frustration, or else they review the past with smug satisfaction, apparently willing to "rust" on their laurels.

The Bible, however, contains many examples of
God's children who had a much better point of view—
those who were never satisfied to relax their efforts.
Consider the elderly apostle Paul. After all his
achievements, he still aspired to do better. He wrote,
"I press toward the mark for the prize of the high calling of God." Courageous Caleb requested a difficult
and challenging assignment at the age of 85. He
didn't ask for an easy retirement. Instead he zealously
cried, "Give me this mountain!"

High in the Alps is a monument raised in honor of a
faithful guide who perished while ascending a peak to
rescue a stranded tourist. Inscribed on that memorial
stone are these words: HE DIED CLIMBING. A
maturing, growing Christian should have the same
kind of attitude—right up to the end of his life.

This devotional is directed to every discouraged
"retiree." Be assured that you can still do many things
for God's glory, and can reach new spiritual plateaus.
Don't wallow in self-pity. Determine by His grace to
"press toward the mark" of His "high calling." Say to
the Lord, "With the talent and strength I still have,
give me this mountain. I may not completely scale it,
but with courage and zeal let me die climbing!"

> *I'm pressing on the upward way,*
> *New heights I'm gaining every day—*
> *Still praying as I'm onward bound,*
> *"Lord, plant my feet on higher ground."* —Oatman

THOT: Spiritual progress requires consecration without reservation.

8. Trust and Contentment

The Christian should be a happy person, full of spiritual optimism and bubbling over with "the joy of the Lord." Confident of God's perfect watchcare over us, we should always see the rainbow in life's dark clouds. Our faces should be glowing with smiles of holy satisfaction because of our implicit faith in the Savior's wise leading.

An unknown author has written, "Sometimes we see men and women who seem to have had more than their share of trouble, yet who go courageously and even joyfully on their way. What is their secret? It is not that their strength to bear burdens is greater than the strength of others, nor that they are more impervious to pain or sorrow than the rest of us. But it is because they have learned to trust in One whose hand is mighty to help and who gives His all-sufficient grace to those who depend upon Him. The inspired writer of Proverbs was doing more than putting pleasing words together when he said that whoever trusts in the Lord, happy is he (Prov. 16:20). He was stating a glorious truth which each of us may enjoy in our own experience. The peace and contentment that Christ gives cannot be destroyed or taken from us by the world. It will not keep the storms of life away, but it will enable us to pass through them without fear." Indeed, if we abide in blessed fellowship with God through the Lord Jesus Christ, we will find peace and contentment in the most trying circumstances. Therefore, when people look at us as believers, they should be able to say, ". . . *the Lord [has] made them joyful*" (Ezra 6:22).

Put your trust in God and His good leading, and you'll be able to echo the sentiments of the hymnwriter, Charles Widmeyer, who penned this triumphant testimony:

> *Beauty for ashes, gold for my dross;*
> *Joy for my sorrow, a crown for my cross;*
> *Peace for each heartache, a balm for my pain;*
> *Sunshine for shadows, a "bow" after rain.*

'TIS HEAVEN—WHEN HE IS THERE!

And He said, My presence shall go with thee, and I will give thee rest. Exodus 33:14

AT the age of 7, I was taken to the hospital, apparently dying from tuberculosis of the hip. Despite constant pain, I found comfort in the blessed hymns my dear parents had taught me. While I was singing one day "If Jesus goes with me, *I'll go anywhere,*" a lady in a wheelchair came to visit me. Taking my hand in hers, she began to weep. Years later I learned from my father why she had cried. Though she was a believer, she had been experiencing much sickness and was upset when the doctor ordered her into the hospital. Full of self-pity, she had complained, "Lord, I've tried to be faithful to You all my life, and now You're making me go where I'll not even have Christian fellowship. I guess it just doesn't pay to serve You!" But no sooner had she been taken to her room than she heard me singing, " 'Tis Heaven to me, where'er I may be, if He is there!" Ashamed of her rebellious attitude toward God, she wanted to meet the "lady" with the high, clear voice who had brought conviction to her heart. Expecting to see a mature believer, she was surprised to find a little boy soprano who was seriously ill and was not expected to recover. The experience proved to be a spiritual rebuke to her. It taught her that she could rejoice and be content in every circumstance, because God was always with her.

Dear one in Christ, no matter where you may be or what you may have to endure, the joy of the Lord can be yours. You can have "heaven" in your heart when you recognize that the Savior is right by your side lovingly directing your every step. Trust Him today.

If Jesus goes with me, I'll go anywhere!
'Tis Heaven to me, where'er I may be, if He is there!
I count it a privilege here His cross to bear;
If Jesus goes with me, I'll go anywhere!   —Miles

THOT: When the Christian centers his mind on Christ, he develops a wonderful CALMplex!

GOD'S UNSEARCHABLE WAYS

The barrel of meal shall not be used up, neither shall the cruse of oil fail.   1 Kings 17:14

THE prophet Elijah had been experiencing one difficulty after another. Finally the Lord told him to go to Zarephath for food and shelter. Imagine what he must have thought when he discovered that the widow woman who was to provide for him was extremely poor! In fact, she was gathering a few sticks to prepare her last meal, after which she and her son would die of hunger. How God delights to amaze us by His unique ways, which are "past finding out"! We may have faith enough to go to Zarephath at His direction, but we're not likely to be prepared for the shock of finding a widow there who is as near starvation as we are. God does not always choose the way that seems obvious to us. He may lead us in unusual and unexpected paths to test our faith.

The fragmentary nature of human understanding can be illustrated if we imagine an ant crawling upon one of the great pillars of St. Paul's Cathedral. What does an ant know of the architect's magnificent design when it sees only the little space of stone on which it moves? The beautiful carvings and ornamental work appear like mountains and valleys cutting off its progress. In the same way, the wisest Christian in the midst of God's vast program can only judge the little space about him. He perceives just a glimmer of the Lord's purposes. His grace appears in bold relief as mountains of difficulty that obscure his vision. Yet God assures us that all will work out for our good if we trust and let Him lead. The barrel of meal and the cruse of oil will not fail. The Lord's ways may be unsearchable, but His supply is unfailing!

> *So dark and all unknown to me,*
> *Except the step I'm taking now;*
> *But light enough when God is near,*
> *To His sweet will I gladly bow.*   —Anon.

THOT: God expects us to TRUST Him even when we cannot TRACE Him.

TRUST HIS LEADING

*Lead me in Thy truth, and teach me; for Thou art
the God of my salvation.* Psalm 25:5

NOTHING in all the world gives us greater happiness than depending upon God to lead us through all of life. Waiting on Him for His direction, clinging to Him in every situation, is the best way to find peace in times of perplexity, loneliness, and distress. As Christians, we need to develop a childlike trust that rests in the all-sufficient wisdom of the Heavenly Father. Confident in His perfect guidance, we can rely on Him to go before us—even when we are engulfed by the deepest trials.

During World War II, the King of England ordered an evacuation of the children from the bomb-torn areas of London. Many of the youngsters had never been away from home before, so they were quite nervous and upset. A mother and father had just put their young son and daughter aboard a crowded train and said goodby. No sooner had the train left the station than the little girl began to cry. She told her brother she was scared because she didn't know where they were going. Brushing his own tears away, he put his arm around his sister to comfort her. "I don't know where we are going either," he said, "but the King knows, so don't worry!"

Many of us are like that little girl. We frequently are fearful because we seem to be alone and uprooted in this dark and dangerous world. But though we may not always understand where God is taking us, *we may be assured that He knows!* The emergencies and problems that we meet each day can be faced with calmness if we simply trust His all-wise leading.

> *Lord, I would clasp Thy hand in mine,*
> *Nor ever murmur nor repine;*
> *Content, whatever lot I see,*
> *Since 'tis my God that leadeth me.* —Gilmore

THOT: God does not ask us to GO where He will not LEAD.

HOW GOD USED A SPIDER

Oh, that men would praise the Lord ... for His wonderful
works to the children of men!   Psalm 107:8

WHATEVER the circumstances may have been when the psalmist wrote this beautiful exhortation to praise, we have no doubt about the great lesson it teaches. It underscores God's providential care and preservation of His people. He is constantly watching over us, and He knows when we have need of His help. True, we must bear many burdens and sorrows, and some trials are left unsolved, but the Lord gives us His grace for all of them. At times, however, He delivers His trusting children in unusual ways.

Felix of Nola, an early Christian martyr, found this to be true when he was fleeing from his enemies. Calling on God for help, he took refuge in a cave. He had scarcely entered when a spider began to spin a web over the opening. The pursuers saw the spider's lacy veil blocking the entrance and didn't bother to look inside. Concluding that no one could have entered without disturbing that delicate curtain of silk, they left, and the life of one of God's noble workmen was spared for additional service for Christ. This early church father later summed up his experience with these words: "Where God is, a spider's web is a wall; where He is not, a wall is but a spider's web."

In times of trouble, Christian, God is deeply aware of all your needs. It may be His will for you to endure a severe trial, but He'll sustain you by His grace. Then again, He may see fit to deliver you from your troubles in a marvelous and wonderful way. Our Heavenly Father is wise and powerful and can use even a spider to implement His providence on our behalf.

> *Father, beneath Your sheltering wing*
> *In sweet security I cling;*
> *I seek Your face in earnest prayer*
> *And plead Your providential care.*   —Bosch

THOT: God's kind PROVIDENCE teaches us to trust in His wise PROVISION.

SHE TRUSTED DANIEL'S GOD

Now the king spoke and said unto Daniel, Thy God, whom thou servest continually, He will deliver thee.   Daniel 6:16

I'M sure you have heard of the miraculous preservation of Daniel in the den of hungry lions. Although the Lord does not always deliver His children in such a dramatic way today, His protecting power is still manifested when a critical situation arises that calls for His special intervention.

Mrs. Dan Crawford relates this true incident: An African girl about 9 years old had repeatedly run away from her wicked parents to attend the mission school. Each time she was dragged back home and severely beaten. But in spite of this, she always returned to those who had taught her to sing hymns and memorize Bible stories. Finally, she was turned over to the witch doctor "to put fear into her," but this too had no effect.

In desperation, the child's mother made one last effort to keep her daughter from forsaking tribal customs. Taking her into the forest, she bound the youngster to a tree, thinking that the lions would frighten the "Jesus belief " out of her. But as the blackness of night engulfed the shivering child, the angel of the Lord must have encamped about her, for she remained unharmed. At dawn a Christian lad found her and noted that the tracks of many lions had come within 5 yards of the tree. The girl said that when she saw the animals, she remembered the story of Daniel, and she prayed most earnestly that God would protect her. The Lord soon gave her peace and the assurance that He would not let the lions devour her.

Let's pray that we might have the simple faith of that little African child who fully trusted Daniel's God.

> *O for a faith that will not shrink*
> *Though pressed by every foe,*
> *That will not tremble on the brink*
> *Of any earthly woe!*   —Bathurst

THOT: He pleases God best who trusts Him most!

"THE OTHER SIDE"

*Let us pass over unto the other side . . . . And there
arose a great storm of wind.*   Mark 4:35,37

EVEN when we go forth at Christ's command, we may expect to face difficulties. Jesus' disciples were in the center of God's will in going across the lake. He had commanded it. Yet they encountered a dreadful storm and appeared to be in danger of drowning. A storm— with *Christ on board?* It seems a contradiction in terms! Would not His presence assure a placid sea and a tranquil voyage? No! It is often precisely the opposite. Life frequently becomes more difficult after one is saved. He encounters fierce opposition and is assailed by a wild tempest of trial. A storm—and *Christ asleep!* Ah, that even deepens the perplexity. The silence of Jesus, the uncounted delays, and the mysteries of our Lord's dealings are often too difficult for us to understand. He tests our faith that He might strengthen it. He delays His responses so that our prayers may become more intense and our gratitude more full when deliverance comes.

We often have needless fears, because we fail to rest on God's sure Word and promises. If the disciples had just recalled Jesus' words, "Let us pass over unto the other side," they would have known they would reach *their destination safely.* They should have been shouting victory and saying to the raging winds and rolling waves, "You can do us no harm, for our mighty Savior is on board!" The Lord had said, "Let us pass over unto the other side," not, "Let us go to the middle of the lake and be drowned."

Trust Christ today. He has promised a glorious deliverance in spite of life's threatening billows and howling storms.

> *Boisterous waves obey Thy will*
> *When Thou say'st to them, "Be still!"*
> *Wondrous Sovereign of the sea,*
> *Jesus, Savior, pilot me!*   —Hopper

THOT: True faith is like a kite—a contrary wind just raises it higher!

163

A PARABLE ON CONTENTMENT

I have learned, in whatever state I am,
in this to be content.   Philippians 4:11

THE English theologian Paxton Hood has written a lovely parable on contentment. He said, "A violet shed its modest beauty at the foot of an old oak. After it had lived there several days, the oak said, 'Aren't you ashamed of yourself, little violet, when you look up at me?—you little thing down there—when you see how large I am, and how small you are?' 'No,' said the violet, 'we are both where God has placed us, and God has given us both something. To you he gave strength, to me sweetness, and I offer Him back my fragrance, and am thankful.' 'Sweetness is all nonsense,' said the oak. 'A few days—a month at the most—and where and what will you be? You will die, and the place of your grave will not lift the ground higher by a blade of grass. I expect to stand for a good long time—ages, perhaps. And then, when I'm cut down, I shall be a ship that bears men over the sea, or a coffin that will hold the dust of a prince. What is your lot compared to mine?' 'But we're both what God made us, and we're both where He placed us. I suppose I shall die soon, but I hope to do so as fragrantly as I have lived. You too must be cut down at last. It doesn't matter that I see a few days or a few ages. My littleness or your greatness comes to the same thing at last. We're what the Lord made us—we're where He placed us! God gave you strength. God gave me sweetness.'"

Are you a bitter complainer, not content to play a small part? Then you too need the true perspective of godly contentment. O to keep sweet, whatever we are wherever God has placed us!

When you're tired and discouraged
And you don't know what to do,
Trust the Lord and be contented,
For His grace will see you through.   —*Bosch*

THOT: If you're not satisfied with your lot—build on it!

GODLY CONTENTMENT

*I have learned, in whatever state I am,
in this to be content.*   Philippians 4:11

CONTENTMENT is never the result of multiplying riches, increasing pleasures, or achieving fame. Even when they are obtained, one finds he still is not satisfied. Contentment does not depend upon things on the outside, but results from *conditions on the inside!* Paul had probably suffered more for the sake of Christ than anyone else (2 Cor. 11:23-28), yet he said he was content. The apostle did not come to this happy philosophy of life in a moment. He said, "I have *learned* . . . to be content." To aspire to unrealistic goals or to grasp at riches that elude us will not bring happiness. Instead, with God's help we must do our best to accomplish our life's task with the talents and opportunities He gives us.

In his famous lecture on "Clocks and Watches," Joseph Parker told this story: A little watch was dissatisfied with its restricted sphere of influence on a lady's wrist. It envied the position of Big Ben, the great tower clock. One day as it passed over London Bridge with this lady, the tiny watch exclaimed, "I wish I could go up there! Then I could serve multitudes, instead of just one individual." "You shall have your opportunity," she replied. The lecturer then dramatically described how the small timepiece was drawn up the side of the mammoth tower by a slender thread. But when it reached the top, *it was completely lost to view.* In his dramatic way, Parker concluded, "Its elevation became its annihilation!"

Let's pray that we may not lose the influence for Christ we already have by coveting something larger for which we are not equipped. Learn to be content!

> *O for the peace of perfect trust,*
> *My loving God, in Thee;*
> *Unwavering faith that never doubts*
> *Thou choosest best for me.*   —*Anon.*

THOT: Discontent makes rich men poor; contentment makes poor men rich!

9. Victory

You may have seen the floating markers called buoys that warn of danger in navigable lakes and waterways. They are firmly anchored in strategic locations where ships might run aground. And, although the waves splash around, these buoys float serenely in their appointed places. The tides rise and fall, but the markers are never carried away. In the ocean, when the great swells come, the signaling device mounts up and rides upon the cascading waves. Often the mighty billows descend, submerging it for a moment, but immediately it bobs back into its upright position. This is a picture of the believer's overcoming life. In God's strength he can ascend with the buoyancy of faith over all outward opposition. The sustaining power of the indwelling Holy Spirit gives the well-anchored soul of the Christian complete victory (1 Cor. 15:57), even though at times he is almost overwhelmed by the fretful sea of circumstances.

A dear friend, who is now with the Lord, sent me an original bit of verse. It emphasizes the triumphant attitude of the believer who is securely anchored in Jesus Christ, the Rock of Ages. This is what Adabelle

Dillabough wrote: "If you can smile when friends are rude,/ Rejoice when you're misunderstood,/ If you can feast with little food,/ You then can *claim* the victory./ If you can weep with those who weep,/ If you can pray while others sleep,/ If when unnoticed you keep sweet,/ You then can *feel* the victory./ If when you part with those loved best,/ And find an 'amen' in your breast,/ You then can *know* you're truly blest,/ And loudly *shout* the victory!"

As you think less of the power of things OVER you and more of the power of Christ IN you, victory is assured.

> *O 'tis glory, glory, glory,*
> *Now the Savior lives in me;*
> *I am trusting—He is keeping;*
> *This is PERFECT VICTORY!*   —*Complin*

GOD'S ROUNDABOUT WAY

Joshua said . . . , Shout; the Lord hath given
you the city.   Joshua 6:16

ARE you troubled, Christian, because the goals you are reaching for always seem to elude you? Do you sometimes wonder how the path you are treading can be God's way when you seem to be going in circles? If you have placed your life in His hands, don't fret. The continuous, roundabout march of Joshua and the people of Israel is a good example of how God accomplishes His purposes in mysterious ways. The Israelites too must have wondered why they weren't sharpening their swords or undermining the walls of Jericho. Instead they were told to march around the city seven times. It must have appeared to be a useless circling of that ancient fortress. They didn't realize that the Lord had a double purpose in this tedious exercise. The heart of Israel had to be conquered as well as the pagan city! It would have been a simple thing for Jehovah to break down the wall at once, but the stronghold of human hearts had to be broken also. Faith's trials work godly patience. *We must learn to wait!* We are not to ask, "Why the long, useless march? Why the noisy trumpets?" It is enough to know that God is leading! Our patience will be rewarded. The happy conclusion is only a question of time. The walls of difficulty will fall by His power and in His own time. Like Israel, we will conquer not only for our good but for His glory.

Meditate upon this narrative in Joshua 6 and learn the lesson of faith. Never doubt that God's roundabout way will lead you to a great and blessed victory if in patience you "possess your soul."

Keep Thou my feet;
I do not ask to see
The distant scene—
One step enough for me!   —Newman

THOT: The puzzling steps of Providence that lead to victory are best understood in retrospect.

HOW STRONG IS YOUR SONG?

. . . the joy of the Lord is your strength.   Nehemiah 8:10
. . . with my song will I praise Him.   Psalm 28:7

THE lark never sings while it is perched on its nest. But when it leaves and begins to wing its way toward the sky, you'll hear its lovely song. The higher the bird ascends, the louder and sweeter its music becomes. Strangely enough, you can always tell when it begins to descend, because its joyful melody gets softer and softer. The closer the lark comes to earth, the less it sings. And when it returns at last to its nest, the happy music ceases altogether.

The Christian too does not have a song of victory as long as he restricts his thoughts to the nest of his own sinful heart, and to the depressing circumstances of his earthly existence. When he thinks of his own weakness, he is overwhelmed and becomes disheartened. However, if he looks up to Heaven and meditates upon his exalted standing in the risen Christ, he will draw near to God and find that God is drawing near to him (Jas. 4:8). The happiness that springs from this close fellowship will invigorate his soul. The more the Christian relies expectantly upon the Lord, the more he grows in grace and spiritual understanding. As he is strengthened by the Holy Spirit, his inner man is renewed day by day. Feasting upon the Living Word, he rises to new heights of sanctification, and his song of joy increases.

If you center your attention on the Lord instead of on your own problems and your own weak self, He will lift you above your circumstances. Having gained this new perspective, you'll "praise the name of God with a song" and "magnify Him with thanksgiving" (Ps. 69:30).

> *The peace of Christ makes fresh my heart,*
> *A fountain ever springing;*
> *All things are mine since I am His—*
> *How can I keep from singing?*   —*Lowry*

THOT: Faith in God's goodness puts strength in the soul and a song of victory in the heart.

169

DOWN IN THE DUMPS?

Why art thou cast down, O my soul? And why art thou
disquieted within me? Hope in God.   Psalm 43:5

CHRISTIAN, are you feeling blue today? You can find out how to lift your spirits by following the example of the psalmist, who asked himself, "Why art thou cast down, O my soul?" You will discover that self-pity robs you of a confidence in the One who has promised to supply all your needs. The answer to the problem is found in that divinely inspired three-word motto: *"Hope in God!"*

Nine boys were walking arm in arm down a street in Belfast, expressing their spiritual joy by singing a little chorus which was popular at the time: "Down in the dumps I'll never go;/ That's where the devil keeps me low." Hearing their happy song, F. E. Marsh said to himself, "Yes, when God's people get down in the dumps, Satan has them defeated. Yet on such occasions the divine Comforter stands ready to give them victory if they will only look above." He thought of the exhausted prophet Elijah, who sulked under a juniper tree because Jezebel had threatened his life. But God sent an angel to minister to him, assuring him that he still had much to do in His service. Marsh also remembered that while Paul was facing shipwreck the Lord told him to be of good cheer, for he would not perish. Likewise Joshua, lying on his face in defeat, was given new confidence when God said, "Get thee up!" For each of these heroes of faith the situation seemed hopeless, but the Lord encouraged them and blessed their future ministries.

Look hopefully to God in your trials, believer, and your way of deliverance will soon be revealed. Don't let the devil get you *down in the dumps!*

> *Never be sad or despairing*
> *If thou hast faith to believe;*
> *Grace for thy duties before thee,*
> *Ask of thy God and receive.*   —Crosby

THOT: A Christian should never let adversity get him down—except on his knees!

DEFEATING DESPONDENCY

*Bless the Lord, O my soul, and forget not
all His benefits.*   Psalm 103:2

GOD'S children who become discouraged and despondent usually overlook the bountiful gifts He is constantly showering upon them. But when they begin to
count their blessings instead of nursing their troubles
or airing their complaints, life takes on a different
hue. The comforting promises of the Word and the
strengthening help of other Christians should not be
forgotten.

The story is told of a gifted preacher who suffered a
nervous breakdown. During one of his periods of extreme anxiety, a friend told him that with the Lord's
help he could overcome his depression. The key was to
practice thanksgiving. He suggested that the minister
think of all the people who had especially influenced
his life over the years. Then he asked, "Did you ever
thank any of them?" The downhearted man confessed
he couldn't recall that he had ever done so. His friend
challenged him to think of one person and write to
him, expressing his appreciation. The pastor took his
advice, and when he learned that his letter had greatly encouraged the recipient, his heart was lightened.
So he jotted down the names of others who had helped
him. Before he exhausted his list, he had written
about 500 letters. As he counted his blessings, the
cloud of despondency began to lift. Realizing that the
Savior had been showering him with encouragement
through these individuals, his thoughts turned heavenward. Soon he began praising God daily for His love
and goodness.

Delighting in the Lord and His benefits is a marvelous way of defeating despondency!

> *Mid sun or rain, mid good or ill,*
> *Through all my earthly days,*
> *May nothing bitter quell, O Lord,*
> *My grateful song of praise!*   —Adams

THOT: If you don't want your joy to unravel, hem
your blessings with praise.

WITNESSING FROM WEAKNESS

And they stoned Stephen, calling upon God, and saying,
Lord Jesus, receive my spirit. Acts 7:59

THE power of God is seen most clearly against the background of human weakness. This is especially true in witnessing for the Lord. Effective testimonies often come from believers who have learned to rely completely on Christ during illness or persecution, and not on their own strength. For example, take Stephen's experience, recorded in Acts 7. In the closing moments of his life, as he was being stoned for his courageous witness, he prayed for his murderers, saying, "Lord, lay not this sin to their charge." That scene left an indelible impression on a man named Saul, and no doubt it played a part in his conversion on the Damascus road.

Some years ago a Christian woman was stricken with cancer. When the doctors told her that she would soon die, she didn't falter but calmly and bravely continued to live for her Savior. She said, "I've been praying so much lately that the Lord would help me to be a better witness and give me a wider circle of influence for Him. This is His good but unexpected answer to my prayer." Many people came to visit her, and she had wonderful opportunities to tell of God's grace. She testified with more zeal and effectiveness in her last months, when her physical strength was fading, than she ever had before.

Do you feel limited or useless because of some illness or disability? Then remember, your condition poses no problem for God. As you yield to Him, He can fill your days with His grace and transform you into a radiant, victorious Christian. Your weakness will only serve to make your witness more effective.

My life was filled with weakness, I was spent;
But if I ever wondered what it meant,
He showed me ere the day had reached its length:
My weakness is made perfect in His strength! —*Anon.*

THOT: A witness from weakness is a witness to God's strength.

"MORE THAN CONQUERORS"

*. . . we are more than conquerors through Him
that loved us.* Romans 8:37

WE face many enemies in this world as Christians,
but God has assured us that we will be victorious in
any situation if we rely upon Him. With our great
High Priest praying for us (Rom. 8:34) and all His
power at our disposal, no one can successfully oppose
us! In spite of discouraging circumstances, we are not
to despair. In the end we shall not only prevail, but we
will be "more than conquerors."

A number of thoughts come to mind when I consider
this phrase. First, we overcome in the strength of
another. No matter how weak we may be in ourselves,
the power of the Holy Spirit within us is greater than
the devil, the crafty dictator of this world (1 John
4:4). Second, we gain a greater reward than any spoils
our enemy ever possessed, for we "shall inherit all
things" (Rev. 21:7). Third, we are permanent victors,
for the Lord God will set up a kingdom that will never
be destroyed, and we shall sit with Him on His throne
(Rev. 3:21). And finally, we are "more than conquerors" because many of our former antagonists eventually become our friends and brothers in Christ. This
happens because the weapons of our warfare are spiritual in nature and result in the salvation of our foes.
By the word of our testimony they will become trophies of God's grace.

As followers of Christ, we may lose some skirmishes
here on earth, but the final victory is assured. Someday we will walk down "Hallelujah Avenue" as "more
than conquerors through Him that loved us"!

> Strong in the Lord of hosts
> And in His mighty power:
> Who in the strength of Jesus trusts
> Is more than conqueror! — *Wesley*

THOT: We become "more than conquerors" by yielding to the all-conquering Christ.

RESIGNED OR REJOICING?

*As sorrowful, yet always rejoicing; . . . as having nothing,
and yet possessing all things.* 2 Corinthians 6:10

IT is not easy to be victorious in sorrow, to be joyful
when we are persecuted, and to be thankful in everything. But this is what the Scriptures command. If we
believe that our good Heavenly Father never makes
mistakes, we will not settle for a cold, fatalistic resignation to our circumstances.

Many years ago someone handed me a tract with
these helpful thoughts: "It is better to rejoice than to
be resigned. The word 'resigned' is not found in the
Bible, but 'rejoice' runs through its pages like a great
carillon of music. There is danger of self-pity in resignation—and self-pity is deadly poison. But we will not
feel sorry for ourselves if we are rejoicing 'with joy unspeakable and full of glory' (1 Pet. 1:8). Resignation
often means a certain mock piety—perhaps uncon-
sciously so but nevertheless real. Joy, however, is not
counterfeit but genuine. It's the fruit of the Spirit
with supernatural power. The Lord Jesus told His disciples that hard times were coming, but that these difficulties meant blessing. And how did the Lord say the
disciples should take those experiences when they
came? With resignation? God forbid! He said,
'Rejoice ye in that day, and leap for joy; for, behold,
your reward is great in heaven' (Luke 6:23)."

Yes, we must avoid self-pity or a "grin and bear it"
attitude. Both are unworthy reactions from anyone
who claims to trust an all-wise, all-powerful Heavenly
Father. How foolish to be *resigned* when we can *rejoice*
that God is working all things together for our good!

I've found a joy in sorrow, a secret balm for pain,
A beautiful tomorrow of sunshine after rain;
God has a branch of healing near every bitter spring,
A whispered promise stealing o'er every broken string.
—Anon.

THOT: The Lord often digs wells of joy with the
spade of sorrow.

THE "REST" IN "WRESTLE"

For we wrestle not against flesh and blood, but against . . .
the rulers of the darkness of this world. Ephesians 6:12

SOME years ago while speaking at a Bible conference, H. W. Cragg told of his experience in finding the secret of victory in his Christian life. He had been waiting on God after looking long and hard at a text on which he was to preach. The more he reviewed the sermon he had prepared on Ephesians 6:12, the less satisfied he was with the message. He looked at the word "wrestle" again, and suddenly he noticed something he had not seen before. Quickly he spelled it out in small and large letters: wRESTle. By thus exaggerating the middle part of the expression, he emphasized the fact that the word "REST" was in the heart of the longer word. This was the key to the verse he was seeking, the secret of the victorious life; for though we are often called upon to "wrestle," we lose the point if we do it with agony—in our own strength. We win the battle by yielding to Christ and resting in Him as we seek to overcome the powers of evil.

It is indeed a strange paradox that "overcomers" do not attain so much by fighting as by "yielding" (Rom. 6:13). As we humbly rely on the almighty power of the Savior rather than on our own efforts, we'll discover that God the Holy Spirit will take over the battle for us. In our weakness we will find His strength (2 Cor. 10:3,4).

Today, appropriate the "rest" in "wrestle," and you too will experience the same triumph as the holy heroes of the past. The victory of faith depends upon the "whole armor" of spiritual preparedness, and the mighty arm of God's strength!

> *Submission to the will of Him who guides me still*
> *Is surety of His love revealed;*
> *My soul shall rise above this world in which I move;*
> *I conquer only where I yield.* —Miles

THOT: Victory over the world WITHOUT comes when Christ reigns WITHIN.

"FORGETTING" AND "REACHING"

... forgetting those things which are behind, ... [I reach] forth
unto those things which are before.   Philippians 3:13

TO be joyful overcomers, we must forget past failures and sins, which God in His grace has forgiven. And we must reach out for spiritual attainments, which will make us more fruitful Christians.

George Burger has aptly commented, "By God's grace I will forget those things which are behind and press forward to new heights. I will, like David, lift up my eyes unto Him from 'whence cometh my help'; like Abraham, trust implicitly in His guidance; like Enoch, walk in daily fellowship with my Heavenly Father; like Moses, choose to suffer affliction rather than to enjoy the pleasures of sin for a season; like Daniel, commune in prayer with God regularly; like Job, be patient under all circumstances; like Caleb and Joshua, refuse to be discouraged; like Andrew, strive to lead my brother into a closer walk with Christ; like John, lean upon the bosom of the Master and partake of His Spirit; like Stephen, manifest a forgiving attitude toward all who seek my hurt; like Timothy, study the Word of God; and like my Lord Himself, overcome all earthly allurements by refusing to succumb to their enticements. Realizing that I cannot hope to achieve these objectives by myself, I shall cling to the promise that 'I can do all things through Christ, who strengtheneth me' " (Phil. 4:13).

The lesson is clear. Never become discouraged; instead, reach higher for the blessings of the Spirit that come only to those who walk in close fellowship with the Lord.

Why not make George Burger's practical suggestions your goal?

> *The future lies before you*
> *Like a spotless track of snow,*
> *Be careful how you tread it,*
> *For every mark will show!*   —*Anon.*

THOT: It is better to look ahead and PREPARE than to look back and DESPAIR.

NEVER STAY "THROWED"

*. . . and this is the victory that overcometh
the world, even our faith.*　　　1 John 5:4

MOST of us don't need to be reminded that we live in
a time of great crisis. There are problems everywhere
we look—not only in the world but within our own
lives. Despair, fatigue, doubt, and many other baffling
situations confront us. It's how we react to these difficulties that is important. As a believer, do I overcome
the world, or does the world overcome me? Am I a
victor or a victim in life?

The story is told that the boyhood friends of Andrew
Jackson couldn't quite understand how he became a
famous general and President of the United States,
while others with greater talent never succeeded.
Said one, "Why, Jim Brown, who lived right down the
pike from Jackson, not only was smart, but he could
throw Andy three times out of four; yet look where
Andy is now." Responded another, "How did there
happen to be a *fourth time?* Usually it is three times
and out, isn't it?" "Sure, but not so with Andy. He
would never admit that he was beat. He would never
stay 'throwed.' So by-and-by Jim Brown would get
tired, and the fourth time Andrew Jackson would
throw him and be the victor." There's a sermon in that
little anecdote, for as a wise commentator has said,
"The thing that counts is not how many times you are
'throwed,' but whether you are willing to stay
'throwed.' "

Take courage. Go forward in faith. In the power of
the Holy Spirit, you can gain the victory over sin and
circumstances. The battle is the Lord's, so there is no
excuse for us to stay "throwed."

> *Against the foe in vales below*
> *Let all our strength be hurled;*
> *Faith is the victory, we know,*
> *That overcomes the world.*　　　*—Yates*

THOT: Think less of the power of things OVER you,
and more of the power of Christ IN you!

10. Worry and Fear

The Bible makes it clear that God's antidote for fear is available to all His children. Since not everyone has appropriated it, however, some believers are not yet "made perfect in love" (1 John 4:18). The word "perfect" in 1 John 4:18 means "fully developed" or "mature." This love involves both a holy life and an unreserved trust. First, you must yield yourself fully to the Lord. This means giving Him your body (Rom. 12:1), saturating your mind with the Scriptures so that you may know His will (v. 2), and casting all known sin out of your life (Ps. 32:5). Second, when you love someone, you do not fear him. You have implicit confidence in him. So too, when you respond to God with all your heart, you have complete faith in His providence, and you believe He will direct you every step of the way (Prov. 3:5,6). Full-grown love casts out fear and expels worry. You will then experience calmness of spirit and serenity of soul.

I like the small boy's version of the old hymn "Trust and Obey." Having misunderstood the words, he was singing lustily in Sunday school, "Trust and Okay."

He sang more correctly than he knew, for everything will be all right if one's life has been committed in simple faith to the Savior's precious keeping. If we trust and obey, we shall indeed be "happy in Jesus," and we will know the love that conquers fear.

An anonymous author, apparently having reached that blessed state of tranquillity, wrote: "When the birds begin to worry/ And the lilies toil and spin,/ And God's creatures all are anxious,/ Then I also may begin./ For my Father sets their table,/ Decks them out in garments fine,/ And if He supplies their living,/ Will He not provide for mine?/ If His children's hairs are numbered,/ Why should I be filled with fear?/ He has promised all that's needful,/ And in trouble to be near."

THE VALLEY CHARIOTS

Judah ... could not drive out the inhabitants of the valley,
because they had chariots of iron.   Judges 1:19

THIS text is a sad commentary on Judah's failure to force the enemies of the Lord into unconditional surrender. Compare Joshua 11:4-9 with Joshua 17:13-18, and you'll see that the all-powerful help of the Lord was readily available. In spite of the enemy's apparent strength and unusual armament, the people of Judah could have won a glorious victory. But instead, abject fear of the "chariots of iron" made them shrink back, and they were only partially successful. Had they carried on their crusade valiantly, they would have found that the superior power of the "chariots of God" was at their disposal (2 Ki. 6:17; Ps. 68:17).

This is a picture of many a Christian today. He can climb the difficult mountains of service and conquer the enemies of the Lord with the Sword of the Spirit, but often when the "valley experiences" come, he can't apply the truths to his own situation. The giant inhabitants of the valley—fear, doubt, despair—seem to have "chariots of iron." O to realize that God has also promised grace to meet the devil's "valley chariots," although to our human vision the prospects seem hard and unbending as steel. How important to remember that the green pastures are also in the valley, and so is the Good Shepherd! (Ps. 23).

How are things going in your "holy war" against the world, the flesh, and the devil? Having won some mountaintops for God, do you still fear the enemy in the valley? The power that helped you scale the heights will also supply the grace to make you more than conqueror now—though you face the valley chariots of iron!

In the midst of battle, be thou not dismayed,
Though the powers of darkness 'gainst thee are arrayed;
God thy strength is with thee, causing thee to stand,
Heaven's allied armies wait at thy command!   —*Morris*

THOT: The fear of God delivers us from the fear of men.

DELIVERED FROM FEARS

I sought the Lord, and He heard me, and delivered me
from all my fears.   Psalm 34:4

AN old Bible that was frequently used by Abraham
Lincoln during the critical years of the Civil War falls
open easily to the 34th Psalm. If you examine that
page, you will note that it is smudged at one spot. It
seems obvious that the rough, careworn fingers of the
great emancipator often rested heavily on the fourth
verse, which reads: "I sought the Lord, and He heard
me, and *delivered me from all my fears.*" Obviously,
Lincoln had come to realize that God is a mighty
refuge. The awareness of His presence had undoubtedly garrisoned the President's heart during his most
severe difficulties and trials.

The more we concentrate on the Lord as our helper,
the more we shall sense His nearness and go from
strength to strength! If we keep our eyes on the
Savior as we walk the tightrope of trouble, we will
maintain spiritual balance and be preserved from the
dizziness of fear brought on by the downward look.

When the famous author Robert Louis Stevenson
was a little child, he accidentally locked himself in his
room and couldn't get out. As darkness came on, he
became more and more terrified. His father was
unable to open the door, so he sent for a locksmith.
But while he waited, he talked to his frightened son
through the keyhole. Hearing his dad's soothing con-
versation, just knowing that he was there, was all
young Robert needed.

In a similar fashion, the Heavenly Father makes
His presence real to us. Through the still small voice
of His Spirit and the comfort of the Scriptures, He dis-
pels our doubts and delivers us from all our fears.

> *Savior, when Thy poor wayward child*
> *Droops faithless midst grave doubt or ill,*
> *Thy voice shall calm the inward strife,*
> *And bid the aching heart be still.* —Hastings

THOT: Fear God, and you will have nothing else to
fear!

181

NEEDLESS ANXIETY

Fret not thyself.   Psalm 37:1
I say unto you, Be not anxious.   Matthew 6:25

A WOMAN told her doctor that she was sure she had a serious illness. He replied that she couldn't possibly know that, because the disease she mentioned causes no discomfort whatever. "But doctor," she replied, "that's exactly why I'm worried. I feel absolutely wonderful!"

Being cautious in the face of real danger is both advisable and necessary. We should take defensive measures against genuine hazards. "Aside from such *normal concern,* however," says Dr. Stewart Bergsma of Pine Rest Christian Hospital, "there is also *neurotic anxiety.* In such unnecessary worry the individual sees danger where none exists. He builds intense, irrational fears which tend to reduce him to helplessness. His distress can become so acute that he is surrounded with what we call 'free-floating anxiety,' a nervous concern that is just waiting for some object or circumstance to which he can attach it and thus widen his world of unsureness and peril . . . . For the anxiety of fear, we are to accept the gift of faith. For that which accompanies resentment and hatred, we are told by the Lord to love. For the worry brought on by sorrow and despair, we are admonished to hope. For our other insecurities, we are presented with the Rock of Ages on whom we can plant our feet to find stability." And these rich comforts are freely offered to every distressed child of God.

Earnest prayer, linked with a vibrant faith in the Savior who is working all things together for your good, is a happy antidote for needless anxiety.

Said the robin to the sparrow, "I would like to know
Why these anxious human beings fret and worry so!"
Said the sparrow to the robin, "I guess it must be
That they have no Heavenly Father who cares for you
     and me."   —Cheney

THOT: Worry can do a lot of things TO you—prayer can do a lot of things FOR you!

USELESS ANXIETY

It is vain for you to rise up early, to sit up late,
to eat the bread of sorrows.　　Psalm 127:2

WORRY has been defined as "a small trickle of fear that meanders through the mind until it cuts a channel into which all other thoughts are drained." The psalmist tells us of the futility of rising up early and sitting up late to mull over troubles that are beyond our control. Putting our trust in God's good leading is the only antidote for this useless anxiety.

Ian Maclaren warned against the adverse effects of worry. He inquired, "What does your anxiety do? It does not empty tomorrow of its sorrow, but it does empty today of its strength. It does not make you escape the evil; it makes you unfit to cope with it when it comes."

A practical way of handling this problem was devised by J. Arthur Rank. Because he did not have enough faith to overcome his troubles immediately, he decided that the next best thing was to postpone thinking about them until his mind had cleared. So when something disturbing occurred, he would write the problem on a card and dismiss it from his mind until a little time had passed. Then, a week or so later, when he reviewed the difficulties that had been of so much concern, he found to his surprise that most of them had already disappeared. He therefore concluded that much of his distress was an unnecessary waste of energy and loss of sleep, for God had stepped in and directed things along paths he had never envisioned.

We can't deny that distresses are real. But we are instructed to turn them all over to the Lord, for He promised to provide everything we need (Mt. 6:32,33). Troubled heart, stop worrying! Start trusting God!

Our God is Lord of earth and sky,
And all our needs He will supply;
So do not worry, come what may—
Just praise the Lord and trust and pray.　　*—Burlew*

THOT: Worry is like a rocking chair—it gives you something to do but it gets you nowhere.

TROUBLED THOUGHTS

*I saw a dream which made me afraid, and the thoughts
upon my bed ... troubled me.*   Daniel 4:5

STILL groggy after an operation, an Irishman mut-
tered, "Sure and I'm thankful that's over!" A patient
in the next bed undiplomatically blurted out, "Don't
be too certain of that! They left a sponge in me and
had to cut me open again." Then a man on the other
side of the ward exclaimed, "Why, I heard of one lady
who had her stitches taken out so they could retrieve
a medical instrument!" Pat, who had just been
wheeled in from the intensive care section, became
very apprehensive when he heard these gloomy
reports. At that moment the surgeon who had operat-
ed on him stuck his head in the door and inquired,
"Has anybody seen my hat?" Pat fainted!

Though this story is fictional, it teaches a valuable
lesson. I have learned it not only from my own experience but also from visiting people in the hospital.
They are often fearful, and their thoughts upon their
beds trouble them. Like Pat, however, most of their
worries are groundless. They spend their time in fretting and disquieting speculations. Then too, when a
believer is physically weak, it seems that Satan takes
special delight in plaguing him with fears and misgiv-
ings about God's good and perfect leading.

Christian, if you are a shut-in, you should realize
that it is easy to become discouraged when your
health is below par. Refuse to let these depressing
thoughts color your attitude, lest you become
pessimistic and unable to serve your Lord. The psalmist, who experienced similar feelings, had an optimis-
tic outlook (Ps. 31:9-13). Like him, put your hope in
God, and He will "strengthen your heart" (Ps. 31:24).

O what wonderful, wonderful rest!
Trusting completely in Jesus, I'm blest;
Sweetly He comforts and shields from alarms,
Holding me safe in His mighty arms.   —Macomber

THOT: When fear knocks at your door, send faith to
answer it and you'll find that no one is there!

WORRY—FEAR'S EXTRAVAGANCE

Be, therefore, not anxious about tomorrow.

Matthew 6:34

WORRY is fear's extravagance; it is paying interest on trouble that may never come! Anxiety drains our God-given energy. This leaves us helpless to face our daily problems and is a sinful waste.

A lady who had lived long enough to learn some important truths about life remarked, "I have had a lot of trouble—*most of which never happened!*" She had often worried about things she was afraid might come to pass in the future, only to find that they never arrived.

An unknown poet has written: "I heard a voice at evening softly say,/ 'Bear not thy yesterdays into tomorrow,/ Nor load this week with last week's load of sorrow./ Lift all thy burdens as they come,/ Nor try to weigh the present with the by-and-by./ One step and then another take thy way—/ *Live day by day!'* "

We should not spend time in needless fretting, for "sufficient unto the day is its own evil" (Mt. 6:34). Jesus has promised us that the primary necessities of life will be provided if we stay in the center of God's will and put first things first. Undue concern about what we shall eat or drink or have to wear is strictly forbidden. Besides, doctors point out that such constant apprehension is physically harmful. Brooding over troubles—real or imagined—may result in the added problems of stomach ulcers, high blood pressure, and nervous tension.

If you are a worrywart, substitute faith in God for fear about the future. One thing is sure, worry does not ward off tomorrow's troubles, but it does water down today's strength.

> *For all His children God desires*
> *A life of trust, not flurry;*
> *His will for them each day is this:*
> *That they should trust, not worry!* —*Anon.*

THOT: Worry is unbelief parading in disguise!

THE DEVIL'S BUNDLES

For they bind heavy burdens and grievous to be borne,
and lay them on men's shoulders. Matthew 23:4

A CHRISTIAN woman who always seemed to be overwhelmed with worry about the future arose one morning with a light heart. She told her family she had dreamed of a great crowd, all weighed down by innumerable sorrows. A host of imps had thrown additional burdens in their way for the people to pick up. Along with others, she began dragging several of these leaden loads until she was completely exhausted. Suddenly she saw the face of her Lord and eagerly beckoned for Him to help her carry her burdens. He looked sternly at her, refusing to touch them. He said, "I supply no grace for unnecessary weights. That is not My burden you are bearing. It's one of the *devil's bundles.* All you have to do is drop it, and you will have plenty of strength for what I bid you to carry." How true! No Christian needs to sink beneath a weight the Lord lays upon him, for God has promised us sufficient strength and grace.

The poet has beautifully written: "One day when my burden seemed greater/ Than body and spirit could bear,/ All weighed down by the load,/ I faltered beneath my sorrow and care./ And I cried to the needless silence,/ As I walked where I could not see,/ 'Lord, where is the strength that is promised?/ Oh, where is the strength for me?'/ And suddenly, out of the silence/ Came a Voice that was clear and true,/ 'My child, you are striving to carry/ A burden not meant for you!'"

Only when we saddle ourselves with the devil's bundles of worry do the pressures of life become more than we can bear.

> *Why do we struggle needlessly,*
> *With burdens large or small*
> *Which God has not designed that we*
> *Should carry here at all?* —Adams, alt.

THOT: God guarantees grace for everything but our worries.

OUR GOD CARES

If, then, God so clothe the grass, . . . how much more will
He clothe you, O ye of little faith? Luke 12:28

THE Bible tells us that we have a Heavenly Father who always cares for us. In the Sermon on the Mount, for example, our Savior pointed to the lilies of the field. They do not toil nor spin; yet the Father clothes them in a beauty that outshines the ancient glory of Solomon's regal splendor. Certainly the One who provides for flowers and birds can be relied upon to show even greater concern for His own dear children. As we put God first in our lives, we can count on Him to supply all our needs "according to His riches in glory by Christ Jesus" (Phil. 4:19). Therefore, anxiety over temporal matters is unnecessary. Let the world worry; our God has promised never to forsake us. Day and night He watches over us, for He never slumbers nor sleeps.

In a large city in Sri Lanka is a huge statue of Buddha in a reclining position. The chiseled face is calm, the eyes are closed, and the head rests upon one hand. A full 50 feet long, the image is impressive except for one thing: *Buddha is sleeping* while the world goes by. He is paying no attention to his worshipers! As I visualized that massive god of stone, I thought to myself, how unlike our God! He is constantly watching to see what we need and to satisfy us with rich treasures from His inexhaustible supply. In His care we are both safe and secure. Shame on us, then, if we are filled with fear and uncertainty. Such distress of mind indicates a weak faith. The Lord wants us to take comfort in His never-failing promises.

If you refuse to worry, you're on the road to being a happy, trusting Christian!

When you see the lilies spinning in distress,
Taking thought to manufacture loveliness,
When you see the birds all building barns for store,
It will then be time to worry—not before!   —Anon.

THOT: God's care should remove your care.

"WORRIED SICK"

And take heed to yourselves, lest at any time your hearts
be overcharged with . . . cares of this life.   Luke 21:34

THE expression "worried sick" is more than a bit of
apt rhetoric. Science is continually making discoveries
which substantiate the truth that anxiety is extremely detrimental to health. Research at Columbia University has shown that even mild worry can affect an
individual's *eyesight*. And an examination of 500
patients attending a British clinic has confirmed that
more than one-third of their eye problems were due to
anxiety. Studies by Dr. Martin J. Shoenberg and Dr.
R. G. Gillespie have indicated that in extreme cases
glaucoma and hysterical blindness can be attributed
to fear and tension. Dr. Leonard S. Fosdic of North-
western University has proved conclusively that
worry restricts the flow of saliva. Natural mouth
acids, usually neutralized by the saliva, are not properly counteracted and *tooth decay* results. One type of
baldness is brought on by chronic worry. Tests conducted at Cornell University Medical School indicate
that the *brain's ability to function* is seriously ham-
pered if one is upset by the cares of life. The powers of
concentration, memory, creative thinking, and the
ability to learn are adversely affected. A survey of
more than 5,000 students in 12 colleges confirmed
that "worriers" made the lowest grades. The Institute
of Experimental Medicine at the University of Mon-
treal pointed out that *stress diseases* such as colitis, di-
abetes, heart trouble, circulatory ailments, and
asthma are all associated with worrisome thoughts.

No wonder the Scripture admonishes us to pray and
trust, and to be anxious about nothing.

> *Is there a heart o'erbound by sorrow?*
> *Is there a life weighed down by care?*
> *Come to the cross, each burden bearing,*
> *All your anxiety— leave it there!*   —*Joy*

THOT: Trust in God is the perfect antidote for fear.

THE "SITTING" HEART

Peace I leave with you, My peace I give unto you.

John 14:27

MISSIONARIES who seek to reach primitive, little-known tribes with the gospel tell us of the difficulties they have in translating the Bible into local dialects. One problem is that many significant words in the Scriptures have no counterpart in these languages. How do you tell of redeeming grace and the glories of the Christian life when there are no words that express the ideas of "love," "peace," "joy," or "happiness"? Many of these underprivileged people live in such darkness and sin that concepts of faith and goodness are completely outside of their experience.

Recently a missionary encountered this when he tried to translate the word "peace" into an obscure tribal dialect. He couldn't find a word that expressed it. Finally, after weeks of difficulty, a native who knew both his mother tongue and the more common "trade language" came running into the compound with the answer. "I have it, Missionary," he said. "I know how we can make my people understand what Jesus does inside of those who trust Him." "You mean you have found a word for 'peace'?" asked the translator eagerly. "No! There is no *one* word, but you can make them understand by telling them, *Jesus will make your heart sit down!*"

Saint of God, are you always in a turmoil of worry and anxiety? If you are constantly fretting, learn to rest in the confidence that you are living in the blessed center of His perfect will, where all things work together for your profit. If your heart is "in your throat," let God make your heart "sit down."

> *If your heart is often troubled*
> *And you wonder what to do,*
> *Just look up and simply trust Him,*
> *He will surely take you through!* —Anon.

THOT: Peace rules the day when Christ rules the heart.

TWO KINDS OF FEAR

Noah, . . . moved with fear, prepared an ark. Hebrews 11:7
I will trust, and not be afraid. Isaiah 12:2

FEAR can be either helpful or harmful. The *Sunday School Times* observed that some fears are vital to sane, useful living. For instance, a man can never be a first-rate surgeon unless he's afraid of infection and therefore sterilizes his instruments. A child should never be left alone until he develops a healthy fear of throwing a lighted match into a wastebasket. Hebrews 11:7 tells us that fear motivated Noah to build an ark so that he and his family could be saved from the flood. This act kept the human race and the animal kingdom from being totally destroyed. So too, if a person is afraid to face death and eternity without Christ, his apprehension is legitimate.

On the other hand, ungrounded fears that produce needless worry and spiritual unrest are forbidden by the Lord. The prophet Isaiah referred to this when he said, "I will trust, and not be afraid." Unfounded dread of the future disregards God's loving guidance and providential provision, and such weakness of faith will leave a believer tormented (1 John 4:18). The habitual worrier, always fretting over things that are out of his control or which he cannot correct by changing his behavior, shows a lack of trust in the Heavenly Father. His attitude is not grounded in faith, and the Bible says that "whatever is not of faith is sin" (Rom. 14:23).

Let fear serve a healthy purpose in your life. When there is reason for legitimate concern, act wisely to prevent evil consequences. But work at overcoming chronic worry and distrust—it's always destructive.

Fear God and the sinful snares of this life,
And in His sure mercies abide;
Then exercise faith in His loving care,
And put needless worry aside. —Bosch

THOT: Fear that leads to faith is constructive; fear that leads to worry is destructive.

I ASKED OF GOD

Humbly I asked the Lord to give me joy
  To crown my life with blossoms of delight;
I pled for happiness without alloy,
  Desiring that my pathway should be bright;
Prayerful, I sought these blessings to attain—
  And now I thank Him that He gave me pain!

I asked the Lord that He should give success
  To the high task I sought for Him to do;
I asked that all the hindrances grow less,
  And that my hours of weakness might be few;
I asked that far and lofty heights be scaled—
  And now I meekly thank Him that I failed!

For with the pain and sorrow came to me
  A gift of tenderness in act and thought;
And with the failure came a sympathy,
  An insight that success had never brought;
Father, I had been foolish and unblest
  If you had granted me my blind request.   —Anon.

LOOK FOR THE RAINBOW

He who shuts his eyes repining
  When a shadow dims the day
May not see the sunlight shining
  When the clouds have passed away.

Only when the clouds are cloven
  By the tempest passing by
Is the rain with sunshine woven—
  Then the rainbow spans the sky!   —Anon.

SCRIPTURE INDEX